LANZAROTE
A HIKING GUIDE

Ignacio Romero

Rubén Acosta y Mario Ferrer (eds.)

Production: Ediciones Remotas and Senderismo Lanzarote

Printing: Lugami Artes Gráficas

© Copyright Photographs:
Rubén Acosta
Cover and pages: 12 13, 17, 23, 24, 25, 28, 54-55, 59, 73, 74, 76, 78, 81, 82, 83, 84, 86, 88, 91, 92, 94, 96, 98, 104, 105, 106, 110, 114, 120, 122, 123, 125, 131, 134, 136, 138, 141, 142, 146, 148, 150, 152, 157, 166, 168, 170, 171, 172, 176, 180, 184, 186, 192, 195-196, 197, 198, 202, 204, 207, 211, 212 y 213.
Ignacio J. Romero Perera
Pages: 21, 25, 29, 30-39, 41, 42-53, 56, 57, 60, 64, 67, 70, 73, 75, 83, 102, 108, 111, 112, 118, 121, 126, 128, 130, 132, 137, 140, 151, 154, 156, 158, 160, 161, 162, 164, 174, 178, 188, 189, 190, 194, 216 y 218.

Mario Ferrer: Pages: 19, 62, 68, 80, 117, 182, 183 and 200. Gustavo Tejera: p. 30 (C.c. y U. e.), 32 (F.t.), 33 (S.c. y S.m.), 34 (B.g.), 35 (C.r.), 36 (P.s.) y 37 (H.h. y C.a.). Nicolás Melián (p. 22), Joaquín García Vera (p. 39), Javier Reyes (p. 90 y 124), Teodoro Maisch- Lanzarote Cabildo's Historical Heritage Service (p. 101), Christian Piesch (p. 103) and Casa Tomaren (p. 208).

© Maps:
Orvecame
Ediciones Remotas

© Text:
Ignacio Javier Romero Perera
Proofing: Tere Perera Brito, Luise Guttenberger and Mario Ferrer

© Design:
Rubén Acosta
Layout: Natividad Betancor

Translation: Samantha Coker

Editing: Mario Ferrer and Rubén Acosta

Copyright of current edition:
Ediciones Remotas
www.edicionesremotas.com

ISBN: 978-84-120264-2-9
Legal deposit: GC 557-2019
Second edition: 2020

All rights reserved. Total or partial reproduction, of this book by any existing means is forbidden without prior written consent of the publisher, Ediciones Remotas.

This hiker's guide to walking in Lanzarote is the result of years of study and fieldwork. It aims to provide essential information about walking routes around the island so you can discover for yourself the wealth of experiences the island has to offer in terms of its history, culture, and natural environment. It has been collated and presented in such a way that it will provide an essential tool for walkers when planning their hikes. Given that nature is an ever-changing force, as is human interaction with our surroundings, it should be noted that some of the routes described will quite possibly undergo changes at some point. The climate and the jagged terrain combine to make walking in Lanzarote an activity that should be carried out with precaution and planning. For this reason, proper footwear, adequate clothing and plenty of water are recommended. The author and publishers cannot accept responsibility for any material or personal damages that may be suffered whilst undertaking any of the hikes recommended in this guide. We trust that walkers will respect the environment and help maintain a sustainable experience of the island's countryside so that it is conserved for the enjoyment of many future generations to come.

General Index

Acknowledgements	7
Use of the guide	8
Part I	12
Introduction	14
Geographical location	15
Geology	16
History in brief	18
Cultural history	21
Traditional cultivation methods	23
Protected territories	26
Fauna	28
Flora	40
Part II	54
Hiking	56
Self-guided walks	58
Walks :	
1-5: Lanzarote north to south	60
1: Órzola - Haría	62
2: Haría - Teguise	68
3: Teguise - Tías	76
4: Tías - Yaiza	84
5: Yaiza - Playa Blanca	92
6: Pto. del Carmen - Tinajo - La Santa	96
7: Arrieta - Haría - Famara	106
8: Costa Teguise - Arrieta	112
9: Playa Blanca - Janubio	118
10: Timanfaya Coastline	126
11: The Volcán de La Corona Volcano	132
12: The People of La Graciosa's Trail	138
13: Historical Teguise	142
14: Montaña Blanca	152
15: Caldera Blanca	158
16: Santa Catalina	162
17: Los Cuervos - Montaña Colorada	166
18: La Geria	172
19: The Pico Redondo Peak	178
20: Papagayo	184
21: La Graciosa	190

Part III	196
Museums and centres of interest	198
Food and wine	202
Accommodation	208
Transport	212
Useful websites	213
Emergency telephone numbers	213
Index of points of interest	214
Index of flora	216
Index of fauna	218
Summary overview of walks	220
Map glossary	222

Acknowledgements

My gratitude goes to all those whose desire to learn more about Lanzarote's rich natural, historical, ethnographic and cultural heritage have made it possible for me to maintain my passion for teaching. I am galvanized every time I see their looks of appreciation in each walk we undertake together.

To all those researchers whose work has inspired me over the years, some of them are anonymous. To all those I have come across as I pass through different towns and villages and who have readily shared their stories, and local knowledge about place names, nicknames and plant life. They have helped me shape a whole host of information I have gathered and which I aim to pass on to those interested.

To those that work in the archives at Teguise and San Bartolomé who have always done their utmost to help me broaden the scope of the information I have collated.

To those other researchers; María Dolores Rodríguez, Francisco Hernández, José de León, to name but a few, whose desks have been strewn with countless publications in a bid to source as much information as possible with which to compile the different hiking trails.

And once more, my gratitude goes to all those who have accompanied me on guided walks since 2005. They have all made invaluable contributions with their ideas, questions, advice and information and in so doing they have helped create a guide that is the fruit of mutual collaboration from which we have all benefitted.

To my parents, Ignacio and Tere, who have guided me and educated me since I was a *nipper* and who have given me constant and unconditional support; not only when I was a student, but also in my professional life. To my sister, Shaila, who has always been at my side, putting the essential heart into life. Also to Luisa, an indispensable part of this personal and professional journey and with whom I share a thrilling way of life.

For Ico and Imobac; know, dream, love.

HOW TO USE THIS GUIDE

Parts of the guide

Part I
This section provides general background information on the island through an introduction, observations on its geography and geology, a summary of its history, its cultural development, the different systems of cultivation, the protection of different territories, and so forth. Photographs of flora and fauna have also been included to provide a visual reference that helps identify some of the different species you will come across on the walks.

Part II
This is the main part dedicated specifically to the 21 hiking routes together with detailed descriptions of each walk, comprehensive maps, profiles, notes on alternative routes, notes of interest and links to other walks.

Part III
This is a section dedicated to providing practical information about the island's resources and services, such as museums, places to visit, transport, accommodation, wines and gastronomy, emergency telephone numbers, web addresses etc. You will also find an index that lists the page references for brief background information about interesting people, places, traditions and events. There is also an index listing the flora and fauna mentioned in the guide, as well as a summary table with an overview of the different walking routes.

Links

Where possible this guidebook gives details of how one hiking route can link with another or tell you about other nearby routes, it also details detours, alternative routes and places of interest. In addition, brief information is provided with reference to the island's history and culture, for example, "continue walking deeper into the *Los Pozos* ravine where you can see some stone walls and railings which protect some water wells. You are now in the archaeological site called Los Pozos de San Marcial del Rubicón. (page. 189)"

Tracks

This guide allows you to download the routes in digital format from the website:
www.senderismolanzarote.com

senderismolanzarote@gmail.com
Tel.: 690 053 282

Glossary of concepts and terminology

-**Autochthonous or native:** those groups of living things which are typical of the area, island or region but which live in other places naturally.

-**Introduced or exotic:** is the term used to refer to species, subspecies, or variety that arrives in a place as a result of human intervention.

-**Lichen:** Is a living organism made up of an alga and a fungus growing in symbiotic association on a surface such as a rock.

-**Nesting birds:** refers to those birds that reproduce on the island and not migratory birds.

-**Species:** a biological species is a specific group of organisms or individuals which are capable of interbreeding and having fertile descendents. It is the basic unit of biological classification and it is named with two terms: the first corresponds to the genus and the second to the species. These two terms together give the scientific name of a specific species. For example, *Euphorbia balsamifera* which is the scientific name for the succulent shrub typical to the Canary Islands also known as the *Tabaiba*.

-**Subspecies:** within every biological species some organisms evolve different characteristics, so after identifying the genus and species, the subspecies is named and this provides a third point of reference to the scientific name. Subspecies is normally used in reference to animals. For example, *Chlamydotis undulata fuerteventurae* or the Canarian Houbara; a subspecies of the Houbara Bustard.

-**Taxon:** is the name applied to a group of related organisms which in a biological classification take a specific name: species, 'subspecies' or variety.

-**Variety:** In the same way as for the term subspecies, variety refers to a collective of organisms within a species which share distinct morphological characteristics that differ from others in the species. So, in addition to naming genus and species, the variety is added to the scientific name. It is a term used mainly for flora. For example, *Bituminaria bituminosa albomarginata*; otherwise known as the perennial Arabian pea or Pitch trefoil, *Tedera* in Spanish.

Key to Spanish terms

-**Calima:** refers to the haze caused by dust suspended in the air that is carried by the south easterly winds blowing in from the Sahara.

-**Degollada:** refers to a defile, or narrow gorge that allows passage between one mountain and another.

-**Jable:** is the coarse organogenic sand carried by the sea onto the shore and which is subsequently swept into the interior of the island by the wind.

-**Jameo:** is the natural opening, or burst bubble, in a volcanic tunnel after some of its roof has caved in.

-**Lapilli:** is a small piece of lava rock or pebble thrown from a volcano. In Lanzarote it is also given the name *rofe*, or *picón* and it is used in agriculture.

-**Malpaís:** refers to the 'badlands' – vast areas of uneven solidified volcanic lava.

Walk information

- Name of the walk.
- Overview of the walk.
- Map (see explanation on the next page).
- Number of the walk.

The People of La Graciosa's Trail | Walk 12

Walk 12
The People of La Graciosa's Trail

Difficulty rating: challenging
Type: circular (return via the same route)
Approximate distance: 7 kilometres (3.5 kilometres to the El Río salt pans)
Approximate timing: 3 hours
Terrain gradient: 380 380
Signposting: no signposting.
Departure/Finishing point: Ye, (calle de Las Rositas Road LZ-202)
UTM: 28 R6465683230688

The walk up and down the cliffs of Famara is also known as the 'The People of La Graciosa's Trail'. It is a steep vertical trail that ascends and descends the Famara cliff face which stands at nearly 500 metres tall. As you descend the cliff you will be able to enjoy the stunning panoramic views across to the island of La Graciosa and the smaller islets that lie at the north of the island, as well as the magnificent beaches and salt pans at the foot of the cliff. This is an area of enormous biodiversity where you will have the chance to see a huge variety of flora and fauna. This footpath was once of great importance as it was used up until relatively recently by those that lived on La Graciosa as their only means of trading goods in Lanzarote. This was a job mainly left to the women and it formed part of their regular routine. They would have to trek up the cliff, laden with their wares such as dried or salted fish to sell or exchange for produce grown in the fields in Lanzarote.

Walk description

The starting point for this walk is the paved car park in *calle Las Rositas* street (the LZ-202 road in Ye) at the top edge of the Famara cliff, close to Finca La Corona rural hotel. The paved footpath takes you west with some steps that lead to a vantage point that affords super views of the cliffs, the lower foothills and the salt pans as well as the Chinijo Archipelago. The downward hike takes you zigzagging all the way, gradually covering some 400 metres of cliff face. You will see the different layers of stratification in the cliff which reveal that it originates from a shield type volcano. The possible explanation behind the formation of these cliffs is that they may have been the result of a geological shift which forced part of this volcano into the sea. The path takes you over a sea of lava from Montaña La Corona

HOW TO GET THERE
By bus there are regular public transport links between Arrecife and Ye.
By road: from Arrecife along the LZ-1, LZ-201 and LZ-202 roads.

POINTS OF INTEREST
- The Chinijo Archipelago National Park.

Walk factsheet

Symbols:

 Ascent gradient

 Descent gradient

 Family-friendly walk

 Walk suitable for joëlettes or specially adapted wheelchairs

 Short hiking trail

 Long hiking trail

 Local hiking trail

"Walk description" - This text details the route you should follow and includes extra information on things you will come across during the walk as well as signposting and brief references to points of interest which are expanded upon in separate boxes.

How to get there with public transport or private vehicle.

A summary of points of interest which are explained in greater detail in another part of the walk information.

A photograph of part of the landscape you will see during the walk.

The location of the walk with reference to the rest of the island.

10

Photograph relating to the walk with caption.

Interesting information related to the walk.

Walk profile which details the start and finish of the walk with gradients and places passed through.

Links to other walks or nearby walks.

The People of La Graciosa's Trail

Walk 12

Orchella Weed
(*Roccella canariensis*):
Is a lichen which produces dye that was used by the ancient Romans, Genoese and Venetian textile producers in the 15th century. It is possible that the presence of plentiful supplies of orchella weed may well have been the reason behind the conquest of the Canary Islands by Jean de Bethencourt.

which flowed over this cliff and generated a younger surface layer which is lower and darker in tone. The flora and fauna found in this landscape cannot be seen anywhere else on the planet as it is home to the vast majority of the island's endemic species. You can see a native species of lavender (*Lavandula pinnata*), spurge (*Euphorbia regis-jubae*) and you might be lucky and see a Barbary falcon (*Falco pelegrinoides*) swoop across your path or maybe even an Egyptian vulture (*Neophron percnopterus*). If you have a good look at the rocks, you will see that they are covered with lichen; this plant-like organism is part fungus and part algae and capable of living on rocks, with no fertile soil. The orchella weed is one such species of lichen which was particularly important in the past as it could supply a purple coloured dye.

Back on the walk, when you get to the bottom, the path takes you northeast towards the idyllic *Bajorrisco* beach set in stunning, isolated surroundings and where a narrow stretch of water, just over 1 kilometre wide separates you from the island of La Graciosa.

Once you have recovered your strength after a well-earned rest and a splash in the sea, you can head northeast to the El Rio salt pans - they are

POINTS OF INTEREST

The Chinijo Archipelago National Park
It became a designated Protected Natural Area in 1986 and was reclassified by the 12/1994 Law in 1994 (now contained in Decree-Law 1/2000) and encompasses two different areas.

On the one side stands the Protected Natural Park which includes the smaller islets to the north of Lanzarote; Alegranza, La Graciosa, Montaña Clara, Roque del Este and Roque del Oeste; and on the other side it covers the cliffs of Famara, the strip of sandy land between the cliffs and Soo and the mountains of Soo. It is an area that is home to the greatest range of biodiversity on Lanzarote and contains virtually all the island's endemic botanical species. In addition, it is the nesting area of important birdlife such as the Egyptian vulture (*Neophron peropterus*), the Ealonora's falcon (*Falco eleonorae*), the Barbary falcon (*Falco pelegrinoides*) and the Cory's Shearwater (*Calonectris diomedea*).

ROUTE PROFILE

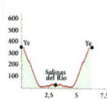

the oldest in the Canaries, dating back to the 16th century. They are an amazing colour and were used up until recently to obtain salt for the fish processing industry. This is a popular haunt for different species of waders. If you look east, you will see a patch of green vegetation in the distance; this marks the spot of the natural Gusa spring which has provided a much sought after source of fresh water since ancient times. The return leg of the walk will take you exactly the same way back; make sure you have recouped your strength ready to take the tricky ascent cautiously and at your own pace. Whilst this is a leisure activity for you today, it is humbling to remember that the tough climb up and down this path was once a compulsory part of survival for the inhabitants of La Graciosa. They would have to haul kilos of dried salted fish up the cliff to take to market and trade for produce from the farms on Lanzarote and they would have to descend once more, laden with their food to return to their little island. This hard task was mainly carried out by the women of the island and we at this guide book would like to pay tribute to all those brave and hardy women.

LINKS TO OTHER WALKS

- La Corona (Walk 11)

- Orzola - Haria (Walk 1)

Key to maps

▬ The route followed by the walk

--- Alternative walk

🟢 Start of linear walk

🔴 Finish of linear walk

🟢🔴 Start and finish of circular walk

[LZ1] Direction change

🔴 Main road

▲ Mountain

⭐ Place of interest

🛉 Lighthouse

✝ Church

The description of the walk continues, providing detailed information about directions and compass points and also includes recommendations on places to visit and historical information about the landscape. Alternative routes are detailed at the end of each chapter.

The photographs correspond to the places you will see or the information given in each walk.

PART I

INTRODUCTION

The eagerness to provide as much information as possible about Lanzarote is merely our way of encouraging people to understand and appreciate its value; for if it is not known, it is not protected and if it is not appreciated and loved, it is not respected. This is why we have spent years trying to raise awareness about every nook and cranny of Lanzarote and its surroundings. It is our hope that, armed with some awareness and knowledge of the island, hikers can truly appreciate what they see when out walking: whether it is simply being able to identify a certain volcano, mountain or gully; or knowing who lived in a certain place and how they used to live, obtain water, and what, where and how they planted crops for sustenance.

An extensive knowledge of the island and its territory will also help walkers understand the amazing symbiotic relationship that has evolved between man and nature and the inextricable link between Lanzarote's culture and its environmental conditions.

This guide to hiking trails around and about Lanzarote aims to provide information on as many different places as possible and introduce walkers to routes which will open their eyes to the incredible landscapes this island has to offer. The trails take you through unique geographical formations created by the volcanoes which erupted as far back as thousands, and even millions of years ago and more recently in the 18th and 19th centuries.

This history of volcanic eruptions gives walkers the chance to explore a mosaic of landscapes which vary from dark shades to light; the brooding *malpaís* of jagged lava flows, open ravines, the peaks of Timanfaya, Los Ajaches, La Corona and the Cliffs of Famara with its sweeping bay of golden sand. It's like a natural theme park that takes visitors through the thrills and spills of the island's flora, fauna and geological features as well as its human and cultural evolution.

In order to truly get to know a place, you need to walk around and explore on foot; in this way you get a complete picture that remains out of reach by car or by bus. There are surprises and delights away from the main network of roads that we cannot see from four wheels, like the trails the ancient inhabitants would once use, but for survival, not recreation. By exploring on foot, you will discover volcanic craters, tubes and farmlands, wander through the villages of the *Majos* (the ancient inhabitants of the island), and walk around churches, castles and monasteries that have been standing for hundreds of years. All of this gives walkers a much more hands-on view of the island of Lanzarote.

The aim of this guide is to offer

An aerial view of the Canary Islands when there is calima dust in the air brought about by the islands' proximity to Africa.

hiking trails that are accessible for most people without great difficulty. To this end, the majority of walks are circular and take an average of four hours, thus making it easier to plan your day out.

The guide also offers walkers the chance to discover the island from north to south with one long trek that crosses right through the heart of the island. This trail has been divided into five comfortable stages that take the hiker from the starting point in the village of Órzola in the north, right down to Playa Blanca in the south (approximately 70 kms). The different stages mean that the each walker can adapt the trek to suit their abilities.

The guide has been put together in such a way that it offers different types of trails; some radial, some linear, others circular, including links and alternative routes which interconnect where possible to enable you to cover as much of the geography of the island as possible.

GEOGRAPHICAL LOCATION

Lanzarote forms part of the Canarian archipelago situated to the west of the African continent. Although it is the most easterly of the islands it is actually Fuerteventura which is the closest to Africa. Lanzarote is located at 90 kilometres latitude, 29° north and 13° longitude. Its location just opposite the Sahara desert becomes evident when there is an easterly and south-easterly wind which brings heat waves and *calima* (a haze caused by suspended dust in the air). The influence of the trade winds, a constant wind from the northeast which comes with cool air and humidity, lends the island a comfortable stable temperature of 21° nearly all year round.

Lanzarote covers a surface area of approximately 795 km2 and its highest point is at the Peñas del Chache (Famara cliffs) which stand at 671 metres above sea level. This low altitude together with scarce rainfall has resulted in a mostly desert island which has experienced significant problems with water supply throughout its history. With an average annual rainfall that rarely exceeds 150 mm, the vegetation is that of an arid climate; there is no tree canopy but there are sprinklings of small woody spiky shrubs dotted over the landscape. It is thanks to the clouds that scrape over the peaks of Famara leaving behind touches of moisture to dampen the island's steep and craggy terrain that, in this area at least, the majority of the endemic animal and plant life on Lanzarote have managed to find refuge.

LANZAROTE DATA	
Longitude	13° W
Latitude	29° N
Surface area	795 km²
Surface area including the islands to the north:	845 km²
Maximum altitude	671 m.
Average annual temperature	21° (summer 24° / winter 18°)
Average annual rainfall	Less than 150 mm.
Distance to African continent	140 km.

GEOLOGY

Lanzarote makes for a superb open-air geological museum which exhibits unique characteristics created by a long history of volcanic activity. The island has not stopped being active since it was first created 14 million years ago and there have been intermittent active phases right up to the present day. The last wave of eruptions took place between 1730 and 1735 and again in 1824. The island's geography varies depending on the age of the volcanic debris around. You have, for example, the ridges and open ravines in the area of Los Ajaches; the black jagged *malpaís* lava fields in the centre and west (Timanfaya); vast fields of dark ash in La Geria and more volcanic craters scattered over an otherwise flat island.

One of the oldest parts of the island is the Los Ajaches massif to the south which is approximately 14-15 million years old. This mountain range that we see today is the eroded remains of an ancient shield-shaped island that had once stood independently in a time long before the island as we know it was formed. Famara, in the north, is another old region which dates back to approximately 9-10 million years. When it originated it was also a shield-shaped islet but

Parque Nacional de Timanfaya.

today we can only see half of it as it was cleaved in half by the cliffs of Famara, probably as a result of a geological land shift.

When climbing any mountain or climbing to a certain height you can see rows of volcanic craters from later volcanic activity which over time joined the los Ajaches with Famara, thus giving the island the shape we see today. These chains of craters are fissure-vent volcanoes which formed internal cracks through which the lava was expelled and which created this remarkable alignment of craters.

In the north of the island stands the Mount Corona volcano, which in geological terms is relatively young as it is a mere 18,000 years old, approximately. When this volcano erupted it created one of the biggest and longest volcanic tubes in the Canaries. Today, parts of this tube have become tourist attractions otherwise known as the Jameos del Agua and the Cueva de los Verdes.

"*On the first day of September 1730, between nine and ten o'clock at night, the earth suddenly broke open near Chimanfaya...., an enormous mountain reared up from the belly of the earth...*" This is an extract from the diary of Andrés Lorenzo Curbelo, the priest of Yaiza, as he bore witness to the historic eruption. It was a dramatic time; entire villages, complete with houses, water deposits, straw lofts etc. were buried, lost forever under the lava flow together with farms and pasture lands.

After this five year period of eruptions, the inhabitants of the island, with back-breaking effort and sacrifice, found ingenious ways to overcome the disaster and explored new ways of surviving on a virtually new island. The farmers dug down to the old fertile land lying beneath the volcanic ash and planted vines, fig trees, cereals and much more.

Today, this disaster experienced in the 18th century provides the greatest source of income for the island; tourism. There are thousands of visitors to Timanfaya, the Natural Volcano Park and the Protected Landscape of La Geria where man and nature have worked in harmony to create a unique landscape.

HISTORY IN BRIEF

The history of Lanzarote is one of survival. Lack of rainfall, low altitudes, flat relief and volcanic activity are just some of the hardships endured by the island and the islanders. Life for its inhabitants has not been easy; oftentimes it has even been cruel, in fact, with the population having to face such horrors as pirate raids, conquests, famine, drought, mass emigration and volcanic eruptions.

The presence of human inhabitants dates back to different periods depending on which archaeologists and historians are consulted. Some scholars, such as A. Tejera Gaspar trace settlers back to the fifth century B.C. Conversely, other authors such as P. Atoche Peña, claim that original settlers arrived centuries before that, as far back as the tenth century B.C. What is certain, however, is that before the arrival of the first Europeans, the island was inhabited by people who were North African in origin, ethnically close to the Berbers, people who had managed to adapt to the island and survived on it. The 15th century chronicle, *Le Canarien* was quoted as saying; *"the women give birth to beautiful babies which are white, like ours".*

Los Majos

The ancient inhabitants of both Lanzarote and Fuerteventura were the *Majos*. They called Lanzarote 'Titerogaka' according to *Le Canarien*. Their lifestyle was based on animal farming (goats, sheep and pigs) and they would also plant barley and catch seafood and fish from the shoreline.

At the time of the conquest the island had a social structure in place that was based around a king, his family and his government advisors, while the rest of the population served them.

Through chronicles from the time we know that there was contact between the indigenous people of Lanzarote and the Europeans before the conquest. Lanceloto Malocello, a Genoese sailor from whom the island takes its name, came to Lanzarote at the beginning of the 16th century and lived alongside the *Majos* for years. The chronicles also detail the arrival of slave ships which stopped off on the island at that time.

The Conquest

In 1402, a Normandy expedition landed on the island under the command of Jean de Bethencourt and Gadifer de La Salle. With only 63 men they managed to agree a pact of peaceful conquest with Guadarfía, the indigenous king of the island at the time. The conquerors, however, committed a series of betrayals and it was not long before a new social hierarchy was established. This was to have an enormous impact on the islanders' lives and brought about great change, not only in society, but also in the island's economy. It went from being an island with

Views of Teguise from Santa Bárbara Castle.

barely any previous contact with the outside world (and when it did, the result had almost always ended in disaster) to suddenly being thrust in the position of being the central axis for Europe in the Atlantic. The conquerors set up camp in the beaches of Papagayo, the city of Rubicón was established and the first diocese in the Canaries was created.

The Feudal Island

After the conquest, Lanzarote became a feudal island. That is, an island that belonged to a feudal lord. It was governed from Teguise, the island's capital, by Maciot de Bethencourt, who became the island's governor after his uncle before him, Jean de Bethencourt. New taxes were imposed on Lanzarote's inhabitants. The *Quinto* for example, was a tax which meant that a fifth of what was produced was for the feudal lord. Furthermore, the Church installed itself on the island and imposed its taxes, so making life even harder. The limited land was shared between just a few hands.

The 18th Century

The eruptions in Timanfaya (1730 - 1735) marked the beginning of a new destiny for the island. Dozens of villages were buried and disappeared: Chimanfaya, Mancha Blanca, Tingafa and Santa Catalina, to name but a few.

A third of the island was entombed under layer upon layer of volcanic lava and ash. Some of the population fled to other villages and even other islands, until this was prohibited in order to put a stop put to a mass exodus.

The 19th Century

The advent of the 19th century brought about a socio-economic turnaround in which the island turned to other forms of agriculture like the cultivation of the barilla plant (*Mesembryantheum crystallinum*) which changed the face of the island. The collection and harvesting of *matos*, saltwort and *aulagas* (*barbed wire bush*) used for burning barilla uncovered the sand dunes. This *jable* sand was then released, as it were, and free to be swept by the prevailing winds inland, producing sand storms and movements in the sand dunes which buried the ancient village of Fiquinineo including parts of Tao and Mozaga. The cultivation of cochineal (*Dactylopius coccus*) also started in the 19th century. Large numbers of prickly pear (*tunera*) were planted to attract the cochineal beetle and these fields of cacti also changed the appearance of the landscape in some parts of the island.

The increase in maritime trade of export goods meant that Arrecife grew and became the economic centre of the island which in turn brought about the change of capital from Teguise to Arrecife in 1852.

The 20th Century

The twentieth century saw the increase in fishing in the Canarian-Saharan banks. Arrecife was the base for the departure of fishing vessels and for collecting the catch. The capital's population began to grow and the fish preserving factories started to emerge. However, this meant that the need for water also increased and so water deposit boats began to bring water supplies from other islands. At the same time the natural water deposits in Famara were accessed and piped to Arrecife.

In 1964 the water treatment plant was built, promoted by the Díaz Rijo brothers. The desalination plant extracts water from the sea and converts it into water suitable for human consumption. This plant and its creation was, and remains today, one of the most important historical changes to take place on Lanzarote as it allowed for a massive economic shift from the primary sector (livestock farming, agriculture and fishing) to the tertiary sector; tourism.

The 21st Century

Lanzarote's population stands at 143,000 people, not including tourist beds, which account for some 60,000 more. With approximately two million tourists visiting each year, the island's economy revolves around tourism.

RESIDENT POPULATION	
1900	17,000
1920	21,000
1950	30,000
1971	40,000
1981	53,000
1991	88,000
2000	96,000
2013	140,000
2018	148.468

CULTURAL HISTORY

Lanzarote's traditional culture has undergone a huge transformation owing to the speed with which the island has experienced economic change. There has not been time to react and adapt and therefore no time to reflect on the traditional way of life and the essence of who we are and how we interact with our surroundings and each other. By abandoning our agricultural and animal farming, as well as our fishing activities, in favour of the service industry, the island has been driven to an unprecedented cultural decline since the seventies. Many farming brands, place names, names of mountains or ravines are barely known these days and many of today's generation do not even think to ask their name. Traditional games once played by shepherds to keep themselves entertained such as *tángana* or *marro* are hardly played at all nowadays and are barely even remembered.

Lanzarote's longstanding and once vital culture of water collection has been all but forgotten on an island where inhabitants once had to employ great ingenuity to survive century after century. Today we can see how the *maretas* water collection reservoirs disappear under concrete and how the water galleries in the mountains deteriorate along with the *aljibe* water deposits. 'Fruit', as figs were simply known, were a basic foodstuff in the past, yet they are hardly even collected nowadays and only a token gesture is made to the tradition of sun drying them to produce dried figs. Paths and tracks which once provided a means of daily communication between villages and farms, today bear silent witness to the empty passing of the wind.

Up until only a few years ago, in any Lanzarote home, with its typical white-washed walls, there would have been a hive of activity, as large families bustled around. There

Water channel belonging to the reservoir at Montaña Blanca.

were many children to bring up and educate, something which would only be achieved thanks to great effort and sacrifice. The outhouse with its goats, hens, donkeys and camels would be just outside the house and would have formed part of a farmer's daily life. Together with donkeys, camels (as dromedaries are known here) were an inseparable part of life in the country, essential for working the land and carrying heavy loads. Today, the passing of time has placed these animals in a precarious position as far as the future is concerned, with relatively few working animals still remaining. The donkeys that work the land nowadays do so because of the determination and love of their owners who do not want to lose part of their heritage. Camels, in turn, have become a tourist attraction in some areas, like Timanfaya National Park, providing them with a lifeline that has prevented their total disappearance. It has to be said, however, that their work today is totally at odds with their traditional labours.

Shepherding, which entails moving skilfully across country to follow and herd sheep with *latas*, or iron-tipped crooks, is a profession which is all but extinct today. Instead, it has become a leisure activity in the form of Shepherd's Pole Jump; a Canarian sport that gives young people the chance to spend time out and about in the countryside and in touch with nature. Traditional games such as the *palo* stick fighting game or *pelotamano* handball have survived, but with only a few teachers and pupils in some villages on the island. Conversely, Canarian *boules* and Canarian wrestling have had a different fate and have endured over the years, having become popular sports which remain deeply rooted in modern society.

DESALINATION OF WATER IN LANZAROTE	
1965	210,000 m³
1971	653,000 m³
1977	1,760,000 m³
1980	1,840,000 m³
1990	5,680,000 m³
1996	10,270,000 m³
1998	12,420,000 m³
2001	16,140,000 m³
2015	25,770,000 m³

Canarian wrestling.

TRADITIONAL CULTIVATION METHODS

Although it may not seem the case at first glance, Lanzarote was once an island that relied principally on agriculture, livestock farming and fishing. Some sectors may be on the wane, but you can see how they have left their mark on the island's landscape wherever you walk. It was once a cereal-growing island with enormous fields of barley, wheat, corn and rye. It also grew pulses such as lentils, peas and chickpeas, as well as other crops such as barilla, cochineal, sweet potatoes, onions, tomatoes, watermelons and melons. The islanders' diet was closely associated with the crops grown, and basically centred around *gofio* (ground toasted cereals), stews, salted fish and sweet potatoes.

Los Arenados - cultivating with volcanic pebbles

The *arenados* are those farmlands which are covered, as the name suggests, with a layer of tiny pieces of volcanic *lapilli*, or pebbles. In the northern and central parts of the island this has occurred naturally due to the volcanic eruptions that spewed out vast quantities of *lapilli* which the wind subsequently blew over the land.

This layer of *lapilli*, which is also known on the island as *rofe* or *picón*, creates a protective layer over the soil, like mulching, and interferes with the capillary action so preventing the loss of water and retaining the liquid in the soil

Aerial photograph of farmlands artificially covered with volcanic pebbles.

at the same time as maintaining a balanced temperature. This capability was discovered by farmers who started to plant beneath the layers of volcanic ash. There is evidence that this method was used as early as forty years after the eruptions of Timanfaya with the production of liqueurs and wine in the Bodega El Grifo vineyard in 1775.

Farmers started to transport this volcanic ash to other parts of the island to cover land that had no *lapilli* in order to improve agricultural production and in so doing created a landscape full of black mosaics across the whole island.

Jable

Planting crops in desert sand might not seem like a very viable option, but here in Lanzarote it is indeed possible. It is a traditional farming method of planting in beach sand of organogenic origin transported by the wind from Famara beach to the interior of the island. In Lanzarote this sand is called *jable*, which probably originates from the French word for sand (*sable*) that islanders have altered and claimed as their own. Underneath the *jable* sand there is a layer of soil making it possible to successfully plant in it. The *jable* has a similar effect to that of the volcanic pebbles, in that it provides a protective layer that retains moisture.

Gavias

Gavias is an ancient traditional method of planting in sedimentary lowland areas and ravines based on collecting and channelling pools of rainfall water. The water runs down thanks to gravity and it is channelled to the land which is closed off with a manmade ridge of earth called a *teste*. The water accumulates, and is then absorbed into the soil and it is subsequently planted upon. There are still *gavias* in use today in Teguise, Teseguite, El Mojón and Guatiza. They are also known locally as *bebederos*, *nateros* or *trasversos*.

Sweet potatoes growing in sandy (*jable*) soil.

Gavias cultivation ditches in Teseguite.

Vines in La Geria.

PROTECTED TERRITORIES

Approximately 42% of Lanzarote's territory is under legal protection in accordance with different ordinances contained in Decree-Law 1/2000 Consolidated text and modification of the Planning Laws for the Canaries and its Natural Areas, Law 1/2013.

Unesco declared Lanzarote and it's group of smaller islets a Biosphere Reserve on October 7th 1993. Many parts of the island are protected because of their natural value such as the ZEPA zones, (Areas of Special Protection of Birdlife in accordance with the 79/409/ CEE ordinance), the LIC (Places of Interest in the Community of the Canaries 92/43/CEE), ZEC (Special Conservation Areas, Nature Network 2000), the La Graciosa and islets Marine Reserve in the north of the island (1995) and many more.

Lanzarote is a precious garden that we should cherish and look after so that we may preserve everything that makes it unique and continue to maintain an outstanding balance between man, nature and beauty.

0- Timanfaya National Park
Declaration: Decree 2615/1974, Law 6/1981
Surface area: 5,107 hectares

1- The Los Islotes Nature Reserve
Declaration: Decree 89/1986, Law 12/1994, Decree-Law 1/2000
Surface area: 165.2 hectares

2-The Chinijo Archipelago Natural Park
Declaration: Decree 89/1986, Law 12/1994, Decree-Law 1/2000
Surface area: 9,112 hectares

3- The Volcano Natural Park
Declaration: Law 12/1987, Law 12/1994, Decree-Law 1/2000
Surface area: 10,158.4 hectares

4- The La Corona Natural Monument
Declaration: Law 12/1987, Law 12/1994, Decree-Law 1/2000
Superficie: 1,797.2 hectares

5- The Los Ajaches Natural Park
Declaration: Law 12/1987, Law 12/1994, Decree-Law 1/2000
Surface area: 3,009.5 hectares

6-The Protected Landscape of La Geria
Declaration: Law 12/1987, Law 12/1994, Decree-Law 1/2000
Surface area: 5,255.4 hectares

7- The Islote Halcones Natural Monument
Declaración: Decreto 2615/1974, Law 12/1994, Decree-Law 1/2000
Surface area: 10.6 hectares

8- The Montañas del Fuego Natural Monument (The Fire Mountains)
Declaración: Decreto 2615/1974, Law 12/1994, Decree-Law 1/2000
Surface area: 392.9 hectares

9- The Protected Landscape of Tenegüime
Declaración: Law 12/1987, Law 12/1994, Decree-Law 1/2000
Surface area: 421.1 hectares

10- The Cueva de Los Naturalistas Natural Monument
Declaration: Law 12/1987, Law 12/1994, Decree-Law 1/2000
Surface area: 2.1 hectares

11-Place of Scientific Interest - Los Jameos
Declaration: Law 12/1987, Law 12/1994, Decree-Law 1/2000
Surface area: 30.9 hectares

12- Place of Scientific Interest - Janubio
Declaration: Law 12/1987, Law 12/1994, Decree-Law 1/2000
Surface area: 168.6 hectares

PROTECTED AREAS IN LANZAROTE

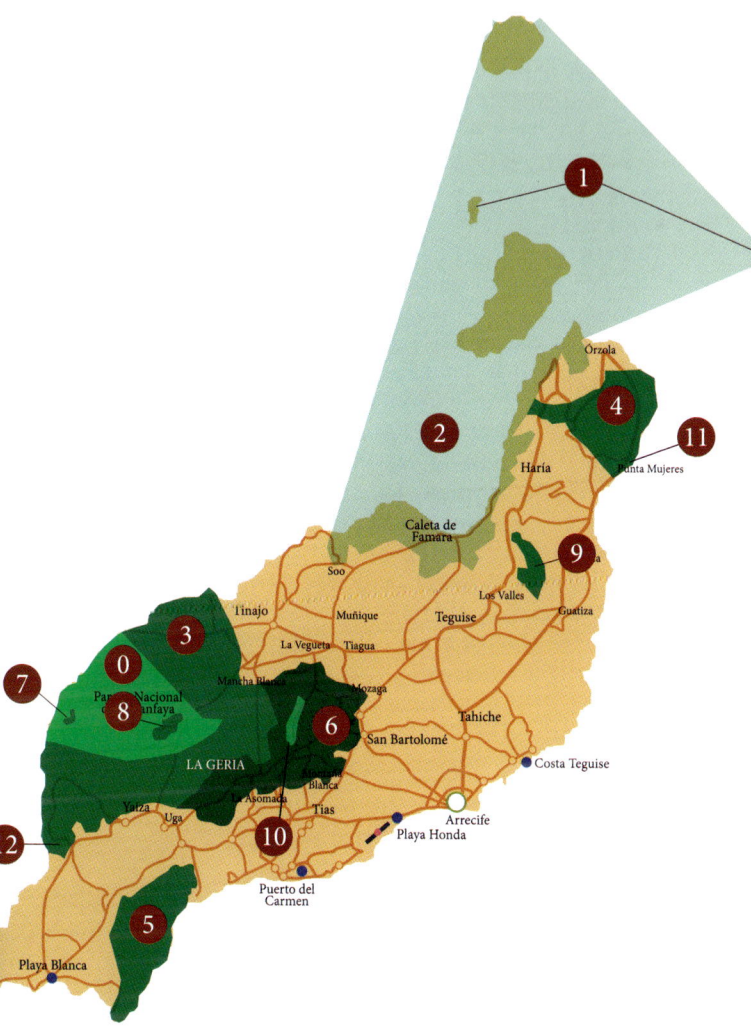

LANZAROTE DATA (2018)

Resident population:	148.468
Overseas resident population:	33,638
Nº of tourists:	3,146,117
Nºpassengers moving through the airport:	7,389,025
Protected Areas:	42.1%

FAUNA

The island's limited surface area, low-lying relief and scarce rainfall mean that Lanzarote is home to wildlife which is inevitably small in size and has adapted to desert conditions. With the exception of one or two wild goats (*Ovis capra*) which wander the cliffs of Famara, there are few examples of large wildlife specimens on the island. Along our walks you are likely to come across both small and large herds of goats, an inheritance from the island's ancient farming tradition from the time of the *Majos*. You are also very likely to see rabbits (*Oryctolagus cuniculus*) which were introduced on the island and are quite abundant in some areas depending on the time of the year. We also have mice (*Mus musculus*), rats, (*Rathus sp.*) and the North African hedgehog (*Atelerix algirus*). Despite the harsh conditions, Lanzarote is now home to many endemic species and subspecies which have evolved through adaptive radiation. The vertebrates are the most visible but also the most elusive as they are quick to flee your path or blend in with the undergrowth - a native species of shrew (*Crocidura canariensis*) can really test your patience if you want to catch sight of it. However, the lizard of Haría (*lagarto*) or the Atlantic lizard (*Gallotia atlantica*) can both be readily seen all over the island and smaller islets as well as Fuerteventura, as can the East Canary wall gecko (*Tarantola angustimentalis*).

The island's birdlife is much more easily spotted. There are many species of nesting birds but it is also possible to observe migratory birds. Some have evolved into different

A herd of goats.

subspecies because of isolation, as is the case with the Canarian houbara bustard (*Chlamydotis undulata fuerteventurae*), which is a new subspecies. It is a particularly stunning bird to see because of its size, its plumage which blends in with its surroundings, and its unusual courtship ritual. It is relatively easy to spot in most parts of the island, although until a few years ago the number of these houbaras had fallen dramatically due to hunting and destruction of its habitat. There are other steppe birds which keep the houbara company on the island's desert plains such as the stone-curlew, cream-coloured courser, greater short-toed lark, Berthelot's pipit, and finches.

African blue tits, European goldfinch or canaries are species that will delight birders and can be found in the north of the island from Òrzola to Teguise. It is also worthwhile highlighting that the island is home to the Barbary partridge, pigeons, turtle doves, cattle egrets and southern grey shrike, which are relatively easy to spot. The common kestrel is the most prolific bird of prey on Lanzarote. However, there are also falcons like the Barbary falcon or Eleanora's falcon. The crows and Egyptian vultures are becoming more and more scarce and their disappearance seems to go hand in hand with the gradual abandonment of agricultural and livestock farming.

Seabirds and waders are more present in coastal areas where there are significant populations of gulls, shearwaters, plovers, turnstones, whimbrels and terns. The migratory birds depend on climatic conditions (wind or rain) but every year the island is visited by grey herons, chiffchaffs and many more.

Even though the invertebrates are the smallest in size, they are most abundant. The island is home to a large number of endemic species, including the blind crab or *jameito* (*Munidopsis polymorpha*) which has now become a symbol of the island.

A Berthelot's Pipit nest.

FAUNA

Berthelot's Pipit
Family: Motacillidae
Scientific name: *Anthus berthelotti*
Subspecies: *A.b. berthelotti*
Local name: Caminero or Pájaro Picuo.
Location: It is the most abundant bird on the island.
Endemic species of Macronesia.

Common Linnet
Family: Fringillidae
Scientific name: *Cardeulis cannabina*
Subspecies: *C.c. harterti*
Local name: Corbato, Millero or Colorado.
Location: Abundant throughout the island although more readily sighted in areas with fruit trees.
Subspecies endemic to Lanzarote, Fuerteventura and the small islets.

Hoopoe / Eurasian Hoopoe
Family: Upupidae
Scientific name: *Upupa epops*
Subspecies: *U.e epops*
Local name: Tabobo, Abubilla, Pupusa or Apupú.
Location: Found all over the island but with greater numbers in central areas.
Worldwide distribution.

Rock Pigeon

Family: Columbidae
Scientific name: *Columba livia*
Subspecies: *C.l. livia*
Local name: Paloma
Location: Abundant in and around towns and is also found in coastal cliffs and in the malpaís areas inland where it breeds and nests in and near volcanic tubes.
It is distributed world-wide. Wild pigeons cross with domestic woodland pigeons, so producing different populations in the island.

Collared Dove

Family: Columbidae
Scientific name: *Streptopelia decaocto*
Local name: Tórtola
Location: Found inland and in tourist resorts. Nesting on the island is relatively recent but it is globally distributed. It is not known for certain if its arrival was natural or if it was introduced.

Spanish Sparrow

Family: Ploceidae
Scientific name: *Passer hispaniolensis*
Subspecies: *P.h. hispaniolensis*
Local name: Gorrión or Pájaro Cagón.
Location: Abundant in and around towns. Widespread global distribution.

Southern Grey Shrike
Family: Laniidae
Scientific name: *Lanius meridionalis* (Previously named *L. excubitor*)
Subspecies: *L.m. koegini*
Local name: Alcairón
Location: Abundant all over the island, it is easy to spot.
Subspecies endemic to the Canaries.

Kestrel
Family: Falconidae
Scientific name: *Falco tinnunculus*
Subspecies: *F.t. dacotiae*
Local name: Cernícalo
Location: Abundant all over the island, it is easy to observe. Endemic subspecies of Lanzarote and Fuerteventura.

Common Raven
Family: Corvidae
Scientific name: *Corvus corax*
Subspecies: *C.c. tingitanus* and *C.c. canariensis*
Local name: Cuervo
Location: Less abundant than it used to be, but can be seen all over the island. Worldwide distribution.

Spectacled Warbler

Family: Sylvididae
Scientific name: *Sylvia conspicillata*
Subspecies: *S.c. orbitalis*
Local name: Curruca
Location: Present all over the island, especially in the north.
Subspecies endemic to the Canaries, Madeira and Cape Verde.

Sardinian Warbler

Family: Sylvididae
Scientific name: *Sylvia melanocephala*
Subspecies: *S.c. leucogastra (sometimes referred to as S.c. melanoephala)*
Local name: Curruca
Location: Can be observed in the north.
Subspecies endemic to the Canaries.

African Blue Tit

Family: Paridae
Scientific name: *Cyanistes teneriffae (previously: Parus caeruleus)*
Subspecies: *C.t. degener*
Local name: Herrerillo
Location: This subspecies is present in Lanzarote from Teguise up to Órzola and also in Fuerteventura.
Subspecies endemic to Lanzarote and Fuerteventura.

Canarian Houbara Bustard

Family: Otididae
Scientific name: *Chlamydotis undulata*
Subspecies: *C.u. fuertevunturae*
Local name: Avutarda, Vutarda or Hubara.
Location: Present throughout the island, but mainly found in the desert lowlands of the south, like the Maretas coast, the centre of the island in the coarse *jable* sand region, in the north in Teguise, Guanapay, Manguia, Teseguite, El Mojón and on the Ancones coast.
Subspecies endemic to Lanzarote and Fuerteventura.

Stone-Curlew

Family: Burhinidae
Scientific name: *Burhinus oedicnemus*
Subspecies: *B.o. insularum*
Local name: Alcaraván
Location: Abundant throughout the island. It blends in very well with the terrain. Subspecies endemic to Lanzarote and Fuerteventura and the islets.

Trumpeter Finch

Family: Fringillidae
Scientific name: *Bucanetes githagineus*
Subspecies: *B.g.amantum*
Local name: Camachuelo, Burrión, Pico Fósforo or Pájaro Moro.
Location: Fairly easily observable in desert lowlands of the central and southern parts of the island and the lowlands of the north. Subspecies endemic to the Canaries.

Atlantic Lizard

Family: Lacertidae
Scientific name: *Gallotia atlantica*
Local name: Lagartija, Lagarto or Lagarto de Haría.
Location: Abundant presence all over Lanzarote, the islets in the north, Los Lobos and Fuerteventura.
Endemic to Lanzarote and Fuerteventura.

Cattle Egret

Family: Ardeidae
Scientific name: *Bubulcus Ibis*
Local name: Garza or Garcilla.
Location: Found in the central lowlands of the island and in Arrecife. It also follows the herds of goats as they graze in the fields.
It has nested in Lanzarote since the 1980s.

Lesser short-toed Lark

Family: Alaudidae
Scientific name: *Calandrella rufescens*
Subspecies: *C.r. polatzeki*
Local name: Terrera, Calandria or Calandra.
Location: The central lowlands of the island, the sands of Famara, Teguise, Mozaga, San Bartolomé, Montaña Blanca. Also present in the south: Playa Quemada and the Maretas coast.
Subspecies endemic to Gran Canaria, Fuerteventura, Lanzarote and its islets.

Yellow-legged Gull

Family: Laridae
Scientific name: *Larus michaellis*
(Previously named *Larus cachinnans* / Caspian Gull)
Subspecies: *L.m. atlantis*
Local name: Gaviota
Location: Abundant numbers all over the island.
Nests on the island.
Widespread global distribution.

Grey Plover

Family: Charadriidae
Scientific name: *Pluvialis squatarola*
Local name: Chorlito
Location: Wader that can be easily spotted in intertidal pools and beaches.
Widespread global distribution.

Ruddy Turnstone

Family: Scolopacidae
Scientific name: *Arenaria interpres*
Local name: Vuelvepiedras
Location: In all coastal regions of the island, beaches and in urban areas.
Widespread global distribution.

Whimbrel

Family: Scolopacidae
Scientific name: *Numenius phaeopus*
Local name: Zarapico
Location: Medium-sized wader visible in coastal areas all over the island. It is a wintering bird which is abundant on the islands from the end of August until May. Widespread global distribution.

Black-winged Stilt

Family: Recurvirostridae
Scientific name: *Himantopus himantopus*
Local name: Cigüeñuela
Location: Found in the salt pans of Janubio where it has been nesting for years. Widespread global distribution.

Kentish Plover

Family: Charadriidae
Scientific name: *Charadrius alexandrinus*
Local name: Chorletijo
Location: Prevalent in all coastal areas, preferring intertidal pools and sand. Widespread global distribution.

Snail

Family: Helicidae
Scientific name: *Theba geminata*
Local name: Caracol or Chuchanga.
Location: Abundant throughout the island. Endemic to Lanzarote and Fuerteventura.

Canarian Grasshopper

Family: Acrididae
Scientific name: *Sphingonotus canariensis*
Local name: Saltamontes
Location: Abundant throughout the island. Indigenous species in the islands and also present in Africa and the Mediterranean.

Portuguese man o' war

Family: Physaliidae
Scientific name: *Physalia physalis*
Local name: Aguaviva
Location: This open water marine cnidarian can sometimes reach the coast in large numbers. When washed ashore you can observe the spectacular colour of their bodies.

Opiliones (harvestman spider)

Family: Phalaniidae
Scientific name: *Bunocehlis spinifera*
Local name: Oplilión or Araña.
Location: Abundant throughout the island. Endemic to the Canaries and the Savage Islands.

Blind Albino Cave Crab

Family: Galatheidae
Scientific name: *Munidopsis polymorpha*
Local name: Jameíto
Location: Blind arthropod with no pigmentation which lives in the pools inside the volcanic tube of Mount Corona; visible only in Jameos del Agua. Endemic species to the seawater lakes in this volcanic tube.

Anthophora (fossil)

Family: Apidae
Scientific name: *Anthophora sp.*
Local name: Barrilitos
Location: Fossils of this long-since extinct bee can be found all over the island with larger numbers accumulated in the El Jable area. Their presence suggests that the climate has changed quite considerably over the course of history.

FLORA

Flora on Lanzarote is influenced by the island's volcanic origins, the very fact that it is an island, its reduced surface area, low altitude and geographical latitude.

It is worth remembering that when the island emerged, the landscape was comprised mostly of *malpaís*, or 'badlands' - jagged fields of solidified lava and volcanic cones, much like Timanfaya today. After 300 years, only very little vegetation has been capable of establishing a foothold and surviving here. In this way, we are witnessing the process of ecological succession; first came the colonization of pioneer plants like lichen, and then the appearance of verode (*Kleinia neriifolia*) cropping up in a few crevices here and there, and so it continues. Some species are airborne, brought here as seeds, spores or via birds, while others arrive by sea on floating flotsam. Thousands of years after arriving and managing to maintain their precarious foothold on the island, many of the plant species have evolved into their own subspecies, differing from their original forms. In some cases, species have been able to survive here whilst declining into extinction elsewhere, resulting in an island that boasts many unique species.

This barren and lifeless island that emerged from the very depths of the oceans by means of volcanic eruptions gradually became populated with vegetation through the arrival of seeds over a period of millions of years. Only very few species have managed to reach these shores via their own methods of dispersal (seeds transported by the wind), others have had to wait for the passing of time or until fate dealt them a lucky break and their seeds were carried here in an animal's digestive tract or in a bird's plumage and by sheer good fortune they fell and germinated. The arrival, the positioning in a certain ecological niche and the way some species have evolved away from their original form because of constant isolation combine to make the collection of flora on Lanzarote totally unique.

The latitude and location in the Atlantic Ocean influenced by the Azores High (NASH) together with the constant presence of the cooling

Famara Daisy (*Argyranthemum maderense*) endemic species to Lanzarote.

trade winds result in a warm, mild climate. The arrival of winds from the Sahara at certain times of year not only brings heat waves, but also seeds, insects and dust suspended in the air. As a consequence of being an island whose highest point stands at merely 671 m above sea level, its territory is predominated by what is called a *tabaibal* ecosystem formed by the leafy *tabaiba* spurge. Nowadays, however, very little of this type of vegetation remains, mainly due to drastic clearance and felling for industry.

"The country is flat and covered with a type of fig tree which blankets the territory from one end to the other and produces medicinal milk." This text was quoted from an article in the 15th century chronicle, *Le Canarien*, it was probably talking about the balsamiferous *tabaiba* spurge (*Euphorbia balsamifera*). The next plant ecosystem that could potentially exist would be the thermophilic forests of palm trees (*Phoenix canariensis*) which would grow above the badlands at 400 metres. In Lanzarote today the presence of this species is sparse and anthropic, being relegated only to the region of Haría and Máguez. The other plant community which could exist would be in the highest point on the island where there is the potential for a lusher area of forest nourished by the clouds swept in by the trade winds. It could, perhaps, be populated by evergreen tree heaths creating an evergreen Myrica-Erica forest. However, this community does not currently exist on the island and if it ever did, which is something that cannot be proven, it may have disappeared because of human intervention. It would have been located in the uppermost part of the Famara cliffs (Peñas del Chache) under the embrace of the clouds at 500-671m. French naturalist and author, S. Berthelot, who resided in the Canary Islands in the 19th century did, however, make mention of stumps of the evergreeen firetree shrub (*Myrica faya*) and the tree heath (*Erica arborea*).

Taking into account the different species, subspecies and varieties, Lanzarote boasts some 700 taxons of plant life. Of these, approximately 20 are endemic to the island and are real jewels of nature. Other endemic species are shared with Fuerteventura, the Savage Islands, Madeira, the Azores, Cape Verde, the rest of the Canaries or the nearby African coast.

Potential vegetation

Thermophilic forest zone (evergreen Myrica-Erica forest)

Basal Zone

Current Vegetation

Basal Zone

FLORA

Balsamiferous spurge
Family: Euphorbiaceae
Scientific name: *Euphorbia balsamifera*
Local name: Tabaiba dulce
Location: Found around the cliffs of Famara, throughout the municipality of Haría, Costa Teguise, Tinajo, Islote El Mojón in El Golfo and in the Las Maretas coast as far as Pechiguera in the south. Native to the Canaries and also found in North Africa from west to east.

Prickle-leaved (bitter) spurge
Family: Euphorbiaceae
Scientific name: *Euphorbia regis jubae*
Local name: Tabaiba amarga or Higuerilla
Location: Found across the island, but more abundant in the north in Teguise, Haría and Tinajo. Endemic to the Canaries and Morocco. Found in Lanzarote, Fuerteventura, Gran Canaria and on the nearby Moroccan coast.

Verode (Kleinia)
Family: Asteraceae
Scientific name: *Kleinia neriifolia*
Local name: Verol
Location: Found across the whole island. This is an endemic species found throughout the Canaries.

Barbed-wire bush

Family: Asteraceae
Scientific name: *Launaea arborescens*
Local name: Aulaga or Julaga.
Location: Found across the island. Native to the Canary Islands and present in North Africa and southern Europe.

Yellow-flowering sea daisy / Tojio

Family: Asteraceae
Scientific name: *Asteriscus intermedius*
Local name: Tojio or Tojia.
Location: Found across the island and especially in the centre and north of the island. Native to the Canary Islands. Endemic species to Lanzarote.

Mediterranean saltwort

Family: Amaranthaceae
Scientific name: *Salsola vermiculata*
Local name: Mato
Location: Found throughout the island. Found in North Africa and the Canary Islands.

Barrilla saltwort (Common Iceplant)

Family: Aizoceae
Scientific name: *Mesembryanthemun crystallinum*
Local name: Barrilla
Location: Found throughout the island. It is thought that it was introduced in the 18th century. Its cultivation was crucial to the island in the 18th and 19th centuries. Present in Africa, Asia and Europe.

African foxtail grass

Family: Poaceae
Scientific name: *Cenchrus ciliaris*
Local name: Gramilla, Grama or Cerrillo.
Location: Found throughout the island. Native to the Canary Islands and present in North Africa and southern Europe.

Sea thorn bush

Family: Solanaceae
Scientific name: *Licium intricatum*
Local name: Espino
Location: Abundant throughout the island. Native to Lanzarote.
Present in the Mediterranean, the African coast and in the rest of the Canary Islands.

Slenderleaf iceplant

Family: Aizoceae
Scientific name: *Mesembryanthemun nodiflorum*
Local name: Cosco, Coco or Coscofe.
Location: Abundant throughout the island. Native to Lanzarote. Present in the Mediterranean, North Africa and in the rest of the Canary Islands.

Canarian fleabane

Family: Asteraceae
Scientific name: *Pulicaria canariensis*
Local name: Purpuraria
Location: Found in coastal regions, near Órzola, Los Jameos, Punta Mujeres, Arrieta, Playa Quemada, Papagayo and Janubio. Endemic to Lanzarote and Fuerteventura.

Verode (Aeonium)

Family: Crassulaceae
Scientific name: *Aeonium lancerottense*
Local name: Verol
Location: Abundant around the cliffs of Famara and in central regions; Masdache, El Grifo, Tisalaya, El Sobaco, Las Cuevas, Las Quemadas, Tinajo, Yaiza, La Geria etc. Endemic to Lanzarote.

Canary sorrel

Family: Polygonaceae
Scientific name: *Rumex lunaria*
Local name: Calcosa
Location: Abundant in the north; La Corona, Ye, Guinate, Máguez, and Haría. Can also be found on *lapilli*-covered fields, on volcanic cones and lava flow and in crevices in and around Los Volcanes, Timanfaya and La Geria.
It is endemic to the Canaries but was introduced to Lanzarote in
the 20th century.

Famara bugloss

Family: Boraginaceae
Scientific name: *Echium famarae*
Local name: Tajinaste
Location: Grows wild in the Famara cliffs area. Today it is cultivated in domestic gardens.
Endemic species of Lanzarote and Fuerteventura.

Famara daisy

Family: Asteraceae
Scientific name: *Argyranthemum maderense*
Local name: Margarita de Famara or Flor de Santamaría.
Location: Grows wild in the Famara cliffs area.
Endemic species of Lanzarote and Fuerteventura.

Lanzarote fennel

Family: Apiaceae
Scientific name: *Ferula lancerottensis*
Local name: Tajasnoyo
Location: Found throughout the municipal area of Haría and in the north of Teguise.
Endemic species of Lanzarote and Fuerteventura.

Arabian pea / Pitch trefoil

Family: Fabaceae
Scientific name: *Bituminaria bituminosa var. albomarginata*
Local name: Tedera
Location: Found in northern regions of the island, mainly in the municipal area of Haría.
Endemic variety of Lanzarote.

Lavender

Family: Lamiaceae
Scientific name: *Lavandula pinnata*
Local name: Matorrisco or Lavanda.
Location: Found in the area around the cliffs of Famara, throughout the municipal area of Haría and in the north of the municipality of Teguise.
Endemic to Lanzarote and Madeira.

Lanzarote trefoil lotus

Family: Fabaceae
Scientific name: *Lotus lancerottensis*
Local name: Yerbamúa or Corazoncillo.
Location: Abundant throughout the island.
Endemic to Lanzarote and Fuerteventura.

Lanzarote red helichrysum

Family: Asteraceae
Scientific name: *Helichrysum monogynum*
Local name: Yesquera roja or Yesquera.
Location: Found in the north and central regions of the island.
Endemic to Lanzarote.

"Mousetrap" Nettle

Family: Urticaceae
Scientific name: *Forsskaolea angustifolia*
Local name: Ratonera
Location: Abundant throughout the island.
Endemic species to the Canary Islands.

Canarian palm tree

Family: Arecaceae
Scientific name: *Phoenix canariensis*
Local name: Palmera or Palma.
Location: There are palm groves in Haría, Máguez and in the Los Castillos gully. There are isolated specimens dotted around the island; Tinajo, La Vegueta, La Geria, San Bartolomé, La Florida, Yaiza, etc. Endemic species to the Canary Islands.

Cliff-dwelling thistle

Family: Asteraceae
Scientific name: *Sonchus pinnatifidus*
Local name: Cerrajón del Risco
Location: Abundant throughout the island.
Endemic species to Lanzarote, Fuerteventura and the coastal region of Africa at the same latitude.

Wavy heliotrope (Camel's tongue)

Family: Boraginaceae
Scientific name: *Heliotropium ramosissimum*
Local name: Camellera
Location: Abundant throughout the island. Native to Lanzarote. Can also be found in North Africa and the Macronesian islands.

Canary helianthemum (Rock rose)

Family: Cistaceae
Scientific name: *Heliantemum canariense*
Local name: Rama papa cría
Location: Abundant throughout the island.
Found in North Africa and the Macronesian Islands.

Lanzarote bugloss (Cow's tongue)

Family: Borginaceae
Scientific name: *Echium lancerottense*
Local name: Lengua de vaca
Location: Abundant throughout the island.
Endemic species of Lanzarote.

Tree tobacco

Family: Solanaceae
Scientific name: *Nicotiana glauca*
Local name: Bobo or Leñero.
Location: Abundant throughout the island.
Introduced and invasive species in the Canaries.

White-flowering alyssum

Family: Brassicaceae
Scientific name: *Lobularia canariensis*
Local name: Yerbablanca
Location: Abundant throughout the island.
Endemic species to Macronesia (Canaries, Savage Islands and Cape Verde).

Bugleweed / Carpet bugle

Family: Lamiaceae
Scientific name: *Ajuga iba*
Local name: Yerbaclín
Location: Abundant throughout the island.
Endemic species to Lanzarote. Also found in the Mediterranean and in the Macronesian Islands.

White-flowering sea daisy / Tojio

Family: Asteraceae
Scientific name: *Asteriscus schultzii*
Local name: Tojia blanca
Location: Found in the lower regions of the Famara cliffs and in the coastal region of Guatiza and Mala.
Endemic species to Lanzarote, Fuerteventura, the African coast at a similar latitude.

Canary sea fennel

Family: Apiaceae
Scientific name: *Astydamia latifolia*
Local name: Lechuga del mar or Servilleta.
Location: Found in coastal regions, especially around the salt plains: La Santa, Caleta de Caballo, Caleta de Famara, La Graciosa.
Native to the Canaries. Also present in northwest Africa.

Zygophillum fontanesii bunge (Canary sea grape)

Family: Zygophyllaceae
Scientific name: *Tetraena fontanesii* (formerly *Zygophyllum fontanesii*)
Local name: Uvilla de mar or Uva de mar.
Location: Abundant in all coastal regions. It grows close to the sea due to its high salt tolerance.
Found in all the Canary Islands and on the African coast, the Savage Islands and Cape Verde Islands.

Traganum bush

Family: Chenopodiaceae
Scientific name: *Traganum moquini*
Local name: Balancón or Mato.
Location: Abundant in the dunes areas. Found in all the Canary Islands, Cape Verde and the nearby African coast.

Sea rocket

Family: Brassicaceae
Scientific name: *Cakile maritima*
Local name: Rábano de mar
Location: Abundant throughout the island.
Native to the Canary Islands. Also found on the rest of the Atlantic coast, the Mediterranean coast and the Black Sea.

Canary sedge

Family: Cyperaceae
Scientific name: *Cyperus capitatus*
Local name: Junquillo
Location: Abundant throughout the island.
Native to the Canary Islands. Widely distributed in the Mediterranean and in Macronesia.

Sea spurge

Family: Euphorbiaceae
Scientific name: *Euphorbia paralias*
Local name: Lecherilla
Location: Abundant in regions with jable sand dunes.
Native to the Canary Islands. Also found in the rest of Macronesia and the Mediterranean.

PART II

HIKING

Hiking is a healthy, non-competitive sporting activity which consists of following walking trails through natural landscapes.

It is an immensely satisfying activity that is not only educational and recreational, but can also prove to be socially fulfilling and culturally enlightening too. With every step you take, hiking provides a fantastic way of connecting with nature and your surroundings. It stimulates all the senses as it allows you to soak up the views, breathe in the smells, listen to the sounds and feel the touch of the landscapes as you fully absorb everything you encounter along the trail. It is also an activity that is accessible to anyone, regardless of age or level of ability, as each walk can be adapted to suit the abilities of all hikers.

None of the trails in Lanzarote demand high levels of physical fitness, nor excessive planning. The departure point for all of them is no more than a 30/40 minute drive away, depending on where you are staying. The circular routes allow you to leave your car at the starting point and then follow the trail which will then bring you back to where you started. For the linear routes you will need to plan ahead and either ensure your car is positioned, ready at the end of the route or consult the timetables and be prepared to use public transport.

Hiking has enjoyed a great surge in popularity over the past few years and therefore it is more important than ever that walkers are aware of the need to respect the environment and all the natural surroundings they encounter along their way. It is only by encouraging a sustainable approach to hiking and ensuring that everything is left just as it is found that we can hope for the rare beauty of Lanzarote to be enjoyed by future generations of walkers.

When following our routes, walkers are rewarded with a variety of unique flora and fauna, archaeological sites and historical buildings and the chance to relish the true unique quality of Lanzarote.

On the Caldera Blanca walk.

Lanzarote and hiking

The modern urban landscape separates us from the natural environment and this often means that we become disconnected and know little about our surroundings. Hiking gives us the opportunity to reconnect and explore places that we may know little about but which are often on our very doorstep. For generations, the inhabitants of the island shared great knowledge of their environment, they were professionals, in fact; agriculturists, livestock farmers, sailors, fishermen, etc. They knew how to value and look after the land that in exchange provided them with food and water to survive day after day. However, these professions have changed over the years and nowadays the majority are far removed from anything to do with working the land. This means that it is now necessary to re-educate people so that they may understand and properly appreciate the land around them.

The sun and beaches of Lanzarote continue to be its main attraction for people in the rest of Europe. Modern tourism trends, however, call for holidays that bring visitors closer to rural life and demand a different way of experiencing the island. It is only logical then, that the range of complementary leisure activities should also diversify in keeping with this demand. The traditional Lanzarote package of a sun and beach holiday plus a visit to Timanfaya and the Centres for Art, Culture and Tourism run by the Island Council is a quality product that has proven popularity and is a valuable resource to offer visitors. What better way to complement this than to link them together with a network of walking routes that can be followed on foot or by bike and in so doing join different towns and villages on the island? By showing and sharing the island's rich cultural heritage, we can return our attentions to the land and place real value on all that it has to offer. Hiking along these paths and trails is a way of salvaging, among other things, memories of bygone years when some of these routes were hugely important to the locals as a means of conveying goods and produce and as a means of communication. In addition to offering a hands-on experience of our surroundings, hiking provides us with the perfect tool to help maintain and conserve the island's natural environment.

Lanzarote was declared a Biosphere Reserve in 1993 in recognition of its natural and cultural values and the way it has achieved a model of balanced sustainability between man and nature. The network of walks recommended in this guide has been designed with these two fundamental principles in mind, offering a new tourist activity that at the same time balances sustainable development in rural areas.

SELF-GUIDED WALKS

This book aims to provide hikers with a useful and practical guide to help plan their walks on the island and to find their way around. By following the routes we have compiled, walkers can explore the island's natural and rural nooks and crannies.

Walkers will need a reasonable sense of direction (and/or a compass) when following these walks so as to be aware of where the key compass points are and where and when to look up and around to see which direction the path takes you.

This guide also provides walkers with details of links to other nearby routes or alternative routes and detours thus providing the perfect tool to plan a day's hiking.

Details are also given of recommended places to stay for those who wish to do overnight walks and of nearby restaurants where you can sample the local cuisine.

The most unusual animals and plants you are likely to see on the walks are also detailed both in the separate sections and in the description of the different walks.

In Lanzarote some paths are way-marked with a system of colour-coded trail signs for mountain paths which can help hikers find their way in some sections of the walk.

Hiking Trail Signs

	PATH CONTINUES	WRONG DIRECTION	CHANGE OF DIRECTION
G.R. Long walk (more than 50 kilometres)			
P.R. Short route (between 10 and 15 kilometres)			
S.L. Local route (less than 10 kilometres)			

Walks 1-5

Lanzarote north to south:
Órzola - Playa Blanca

Difficulty rating: moderate
Type: linear
Approximate distance: 67 kms
Approximate timing: 15 hours

These walks provide a series of treks which reveal the island's stunning interior from the northernmost point in Órzola to the tourist resort of Playa Blanca in the south. They take you through a landscape full of contrasts; volcanic landscapes juxtapose with sandy plains and white-washed villages contrast with dark farmlands. It is also a route replete with unique plants and wildlife, and a history unlike any place else. This north-south route takes in towns and villages like Haría, Teguise, San Bartolomé, Tías, Uga and Yaiza ansd showcases natural phenomena such as volcanic tubes, malpaís badlands that date from different eras, volcanic sand and pebbles. These walks also encompass La Geria: Lanzarote's other-worldly garden.

ROUTE PROFILE

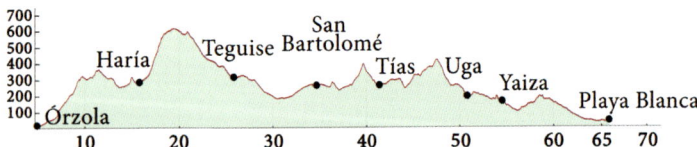

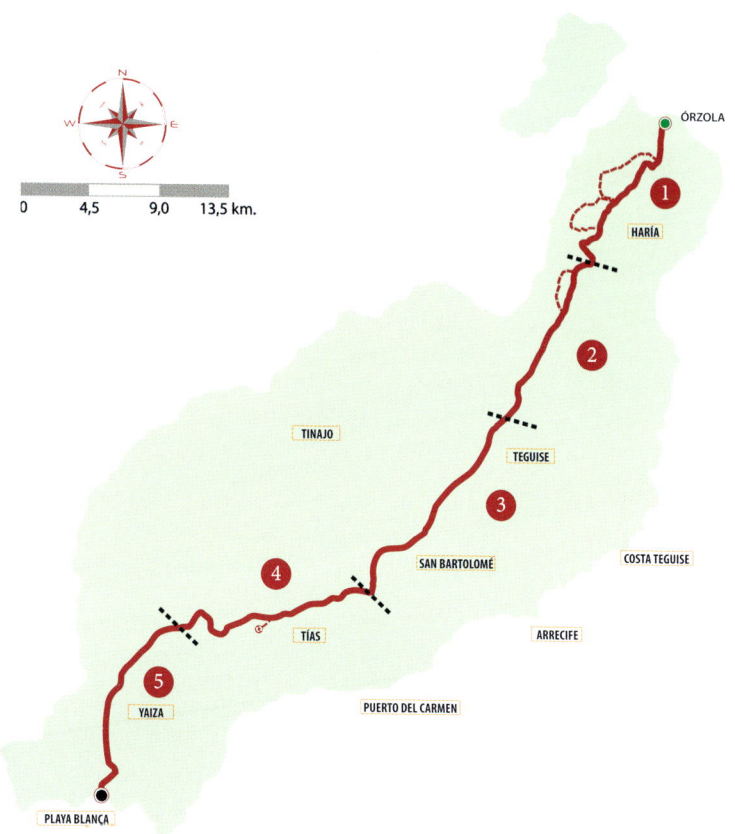

In this guide we divide the north to south route into five stages so that it is more comfortable and allows time to soak up the island's surroundings and fully appreciate the landscapes, architecture and people.

Walk 1.- **Órzola-Haría**
Walk 2.- **Haría-Teguise**
Walk 3.- **Teguise-Tías**
Walk 4.- **Tías-Yaiza**
Walk 5.- **Yaiza-Playa Blanca**

For the more demanding hiker who likes a challenge, this walk could be covered in two stages with the midway stop-off-point being the town of San Bartolomé, at the island's geographical centre. Accommodation can be found in the town itself or in the surrounding villages of Mozaga, El Islote, La Florida, Montaña Blanca, for example.

1.- **Órzola - San Bartolomé** (Walks 1, 2 and half of 3).
2.- **San Bartolomé - Playa Blanca** (half of Walk 3 and 4 & 5).

Walk 1

Lanzarote from north to south: Órzola - Haría

Difficulty rating: moderate
Type: linear
Approximate distance: 13 kilometres
Approximate timing: 3 hrs 30 minutes
Terrain gradient: 590 ▲ 230 ▲
Signposting: only one section marked as a long 'GR' route (GR131) with white and red stripes. Others are marked as short, or 'PR' routes with white and yellow stripes.

Departure point: Órzola harbour
UTM: 28R6504273233742
Finishing point: Plaza de Haría square
UTM: 28R6459303225141
Suitable for families with children and users of joëlettes or specially adapted wheelchairs.

The starting point is the coastal village of Órzola at the northern tip of the island and the main link with the nearby island of La Graciosa. The proposed walk passes through vineyards and volcanic craters and the slopes of the La Quemada and Montaña Corona mountains. It is a rough and dark terrain scattered with spurge shrubs and endemic succulents. This striking landscape is marked by the spectacular blanket of vivid greens and yellows of the lichen that stand out against the otherwise black sea of lava.

The walk finishes by bringing you into the two sister villages of Máguez and Haría, which are instantly recognizable by their plentiful palm trees that provide green relief in the middle of an otherwise desert landscape.

Walk 1

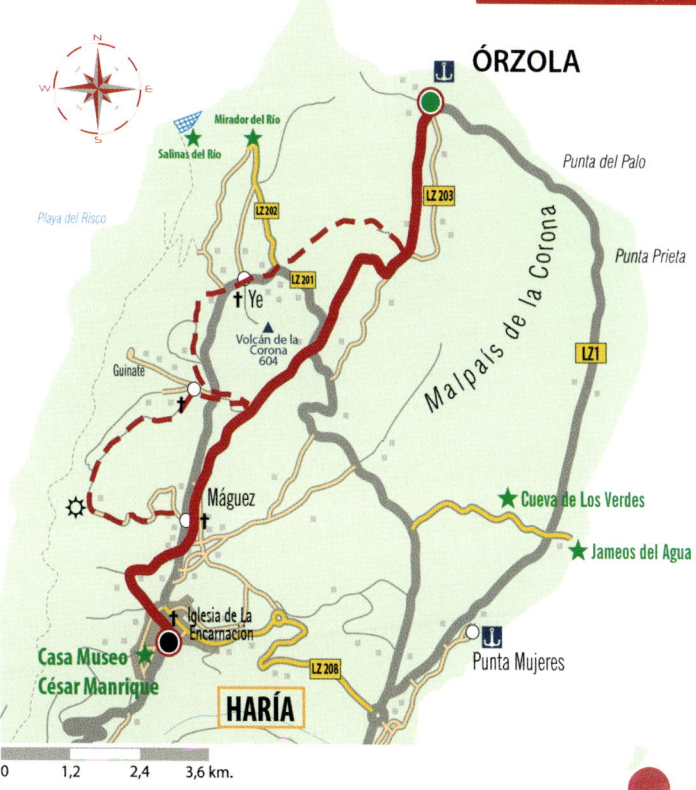

Walk description

This walk starts in Órzola at 0 metres above sea level. This is the coastal village that provides the ferry connection with the island of la Graciosa. You can hop on a ferry and barely 30 minutes later disembark on the eighth Canary Island. From Órzola harbour you can start heading south, down La *Quemadita* road. When you get to the crossroads with the *Playa de la Cantería* Road, follow the path along the ravine heading southwest. Keep walking along this ravine ignoring any branches in different directions, just keep heading south. You will pass an outcrop of basalt rocks known as Peña Jendía. Some parts of this ravine are rocky and to the side of us there are some sandy fields. Keep walking and you get to some aloe vera plantations belonging to the aloe producers Lanzaloe. Keep heading south and start a slight zigzag uphill stretch called Lomo

HOW TO GET THERE

By bus: there are regular public transport links between Arrecife and Órzola.
By road: from Arrecife along the LZ-1 road.

PLACES OF INTEREST

- Paleontological site in Órzola (continued overleaf)

Órzola - Haría

- Natural Monument of La Corona
- The Encarnación Church
- César Manrique House-Museum

'My joy at living and constantly creating is born of having studied, contemplated and loved the great wisdom of nature'

César Manrique
Escrito en el fuego

Blanco which takes you to a lava field. Once on the LZ-203 asphalt road, walk parallel heading west up to a fork in the road with a dirt road to the right. At this point you have a choice of routes to follow (see page 66). You can opt for the route that takes you through the villages of Ye and Guinate or continue along the road and take the second turning on the right, just in front of an old tool shed. The path takes you uphill between two stone walls. This area, called Lajares, has a distinctive appearance because of the combination of the volcanic rock walls that protect the vines from the prevailing wind and the rows of prickly pear cactus plants which are cultivated for their fruit.

As this path ascends it automatically takes you south towards the LZ-201 road. Be careful as you walk along this road as there is no verge. Keep going until you get to the first bend in the road and then exit along the dirt path opposite. You are now walking along the foot of the *Volcán de la Corona* volcano (see Walk 11), one of the island's most spectacular volcanoes which created the enormous area of lava badlands known as the Malpaís de la Corona. This area together with the volcano itself, is a protected natural park and has been designated a Natural Monument. This is where the island's longest

Walk 1

ROUTE PROFILE

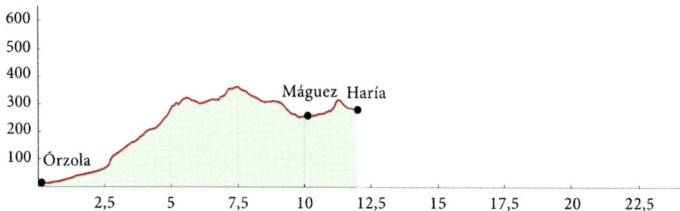

volcanic tube starts and descends all the way down to the sea. The Cueva de los Verdes caves and the Jameos del Agua tourist attractions are two parts of the same tunnel which were adapted by the artists César Manrique and Jesús Soto for tourist visits.

As you continue south, you will see a big manmade *alcogida* water collection reservoir made to capture the rain water and channel it to a nearby underground water deposit called an *aljibe*. Just 600 metres further on you can choose to follow another route called the Gayo Walk (page 66) which takes you west just after the *aljibe*.

Still heading south, stay on the path which takes you directly to Maguez along *calle Cuervo* street. This is a typical old village and home to famous Canarian wrestlers and stick fighters. Head down *Las Casillas* street and turn right into *A. Curbelo "Nicolás, el de la guagua"* street which leads you to the Santa Bárbara church. Built in 1974, this was the work of César Manrique and architect, Fernando Higueras, who took the old chapel as inspiration, but designed it to a larger scale. This is Manrique's only religious building and he also designed and made the mural that hangs behind the main altar. You can leave Máguez along *San Pedro* street or *Santa Bárbara* street and then go along *calle la Tahoyo* street. This soon turns into *calle Romero* street and you are now in Haría.

Enter the village of Haría along *calle La Cilla* street which takes you to the main square (283

LINKS WITH OTHER WALKS

- Mount Corona (Walk 11)

- "Camino de los Gracioseros" - The Graciosa People's Route (Walk 12)

65

metres above sea level) which is the village's nerve centre overlooked by the La Encarnación church. You have arrived at the end of the route.

Alternative routes

Via Ye and Guinate (6.5 kms). From the fork in the LZ-203 road which you were walking parallel along, turn west along a dirt path which ascends steeply up the side of the La Quemada de Órzola volcano. Once at the top, walk along the Vega Grande de Ye plain and then another climb takes you to the smaller plain, the Vega Chica de Ye. There is just one more climb to go that finally takes you to the village of Ye which you cross into along the *calle San Francisco Javier* (LZ-201). Before reaching the church of the same name you can see the start of the hike that takes you up Mount Corona (see Walk 11). Pass the church and keep going until the last house, then take the volcanic pebbly path alongside the house. The ascent is quite challenging, flanked by Canary sorrel bushes, and leads to the region of Guatifay. The path continues south until you can see the village of Guinate where you need to find the volcanic pebble path which descends into the village. Once you are in the main street, *La Majadita,* turn eastwards and leave the village, crossing the LZ-201 and go along a dirt path which takes you to the original route heading south towards Máguez.

Via Gayo (6 kms). From where the road to the entrance of the Guinate village meets the LZ-201 there is a slope to the southwest which you need to climb and follow until you reach Máguez. This dirt path affords magnificent views of the north of the island and across to the Chinijo Archipelago and the area known as Rincón de Guinate. You will also see two holes of about a metre deep; these are the Gayo springs. As you turn east, the path turns to asphalt and you start to head down to Máguez along *calle La Caldera* street. You are now back on the Órzola-Haría route heading south.

POINTS OF INTEREST

Paleontological site in Órzola

If you follow *calle Playa de la Cantería* street in Órzola, you reach the beach of the same name. Look up and you will see a path that leads towards the cliff and takes you to the paleontological site located in the Valle Chico valley. This site, together with that of the Valle Grande, another valley to the south, is home to some fossilised *Ratite eggs*. These are ancient birds related to the ostrich. The egg fossils are in a sedimentary layer of organogenic sand dating back millions of years. Scientists are still theorising as to the origin of these flightless bird fossils.

Mount Corona Natural Monument

This is a Protected Natural Space which harbours the Volcán de la Corona volcanic cone and its *malpaís* lava fields (badlands). The land encompassed in this protected area is an important part of the island's history as it reveals how vegetation eventually colonized the lava flows that spewed out of the volcano some 18,000 years ago. It also harbours a well-developed layer of *tabaiba* spurge shrublands and a spectacular volcanic crater from which an extensive volcanic tube runs right down to the sea.

César Manrique (1919-1992)

Lanzarote-born artist who played an important role in protecting the island's environment in the early days of its tourism and construction boom. He was also the genius and creative power behind the Centres of Arts, Culture and Tourism that belong to the *Cabildo*, the local island council. They comprise the Jameos del Agua, Mirador del Río, Monument to the Farm worker, El Diablo restaurant in Timanfaya, the Cactus Garden and the MIAC Contemporary Art Museum. He was an artist who was skilled in painting, sculpture, architecture and design. He also created the distinctive wind sculptures that can be seen on several roundabouts across the island. Today his Foundation invites visitors to discover more about his life and works in his former homes in the Taro of Tahíche and in the House-Museum in Haría.

Walk 2 — Lanzarote from north to south: Haría - Teguise

Difficulty rating: moderate
Type: linear
Approximate distance: 12 kilometres
Approximate timing: 3 hrs 30 minutes
Terrain elevation: 378 ▲ 354 ▲
Signposting: only one section marked as a long 'GR' route (GR131) with white and red stripes. Others are marked as short, or 'PR' routes with white and yellow stripes.

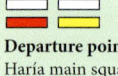

Departure point: Haría main square
UTM: 28 R6459303225141
Finishing point: Plaza de la Constitución square
UTM: 28 R6401763215411

This is one of the island's most outstanding walks and it links two important villages; Haría with its quaint old buildings and palm trees and the Villa of Teguise whose cobbled streets and colonial buildings are steeped in history. The route takes you up the *Malpaso* slopes, one of the island's greenest hillsides and home to abundant endemic plant life and a reforested pine grove where a wide variety of birdlife take shelter. It also takes you past the highest point above sea level, the *Peñas del Chache* (671 m) and alongside the chapel of the former patron saint of the island, the Virgen de las Nieves.

The walk concludes in the Villa of Teguise, which was the island's former capital and centre of all civil, military, economic and ecclesiastic power until 1852. It was the historical feudal capital and centre of tax collection, thus making it a magnet for multiple pirate attacks in the past.

Walk 2

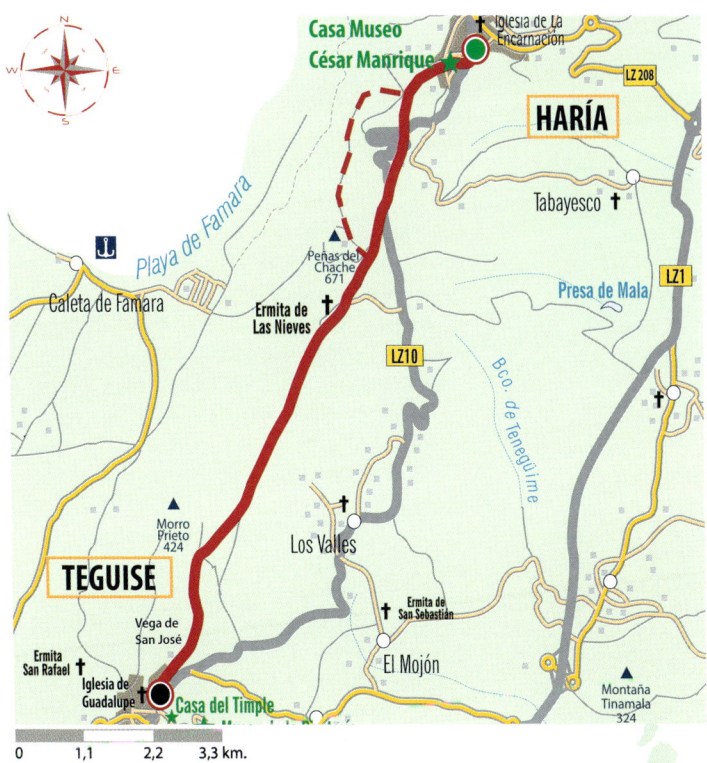

Walk description

The starting point is *the León y Castillo* plaza in Haría which stands at 283m above sea level. It is a picture-postcard pretty square and nerve centre of this northern oasis. Head southwest towards the *Plaza de la Constitución* square and the town hall where you can choose to join the Haría-Famara walk if you wish. If not, keep going just 20 metres along *calle La Longuera* street and take the left turn into *César Manrique* street. When this street almost comes to an end, you will see that you pass the César Manrique House-Museum (see page 67) which was this much-mourned artist's former home. A little further on you will see the palm weaving workshop of the artisan Eulogio, one of the last traditional basket weavers on the island. Haría is one of the few villages where this traditional handicraft endures,

HOW TO GET THERE

By bus: there are regular public transport links between Arrecife and Haría.
By road: from Arrecife along the LZ-1 and LZ-10

PLACES OF INTEREST

- The Encarnación Church
(continued overleaf)

- César Manrique House-Museum
- The Las Nieves chapel
- The Ermita de San José Chapel and Farmstead Ruins
- The historical town of Teguise

'The island itself is a sublime work of art, its mountains, volcanoes, farmlands, saltpans, vineyards, marinas, and silent soothing winds comprise the alphabet that spells out the shapes and concepts I use as a sculptor.'

Pancho Lasso
quoted by Agustín de la Hoz in the book Lancelot, *Obra periodística 1981-1988* - a compilation of his articles and essays published in Lancelot magazine.

but it was once a more widespread craft which produced much sought-after baskets, hats, mats etc. Back on the walk, as you leave Haría behind you, turn right at the fork and head southwest along the so-called Royal Malpaso Walk (*Camino Real de Malpaso*). This route is interrupted by the LZ-10 dual carriageway, but it does not stop you from admiring the vegetation along the way, such as the endemic verode succulent (*Aeonium lancerottense*), the yellow flowered endemic tojio (*Asteriscus intermedius*), the Arabian pea (*Bituminaria bituminosa*), the shrubby Carlina salcifolia thistle and in winter the fennel-like *tajasnoyos* (*Ferula lancerottensis*), as well as Famara daisies (*Argyranthemun maderense*) and even giant buttercups (*Ranunculus cosrtusfolius*) which grow in some shady crevices. You will need to cross the LZ-10 and follow the paved path directly opposite on the other side of the road until you have to cross the LZ-10 again. Cross and in front of you there is a huge stone and concrete wall which is one of the road's bends. Just here the path zigzags and crosses the LZ-10 once more. Cross and head southeast along a path with steps and keep going until you can see the vast Temisa ravine. The path takes you up in a south westerly direction until you need to cross the LZ-10 for the last time and continue south. The path turns into a dirt track again and takes you between the sandy crop fields at the

Walk 2

ROUTE PROFILE

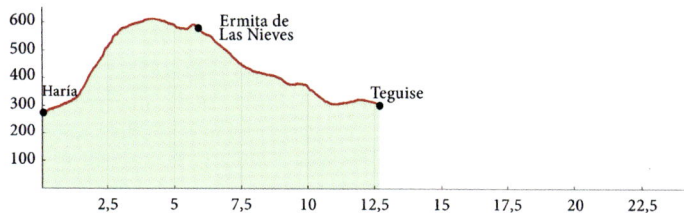

highest point of the island where mostly potatoes (*Solanum tuberosum*) are grown.

You will reach a crossroads (to the left is the LZ-10 and to the northeast is the Los Helechos restaurant.) You should continue south along an asphalted path which soon leads to a fork where you need to take the left-hand path southwards. The path to the right takes you to the *Bosquecillo*, or 'little forest' where you can join the Arrieta - Haría -Famara walk if you wish.

Back on the asphalt path heading south you can see a military radar installation to the right which is strategically placed on the island's highest mountain range, the *Peñas del Chache* (671m). The asphalt path comes to an end but you should still head south and keep the Las Nieves chapel in your sights. The Virgin of Las Nieves was the former patron saint of Lanzarote and this chapel was once the centre of great devotion and religious fervour. To the right you pass the enormous La Poceta, or Rincón de la Paja ravine which forms part of the descent on the Arrieta-Haría-Famara walk. Keep heading south and you will pass some more military installations. This dirt track takes you all the way to Teguise. To the south you will see the Santa Bárbara Castle sitting on top of Mount Guanapay. This was an ancient look-out fortress which now houses the Pirate Museum. (See page 150).

If you feel ready for a shortcut and wish to shorten the hike, you need to follow a footpath to the right which takes you across half of the *Vega de San José* plain and passes through the ruins

LINKS WITH OTHER WALKS

- Arrieta - Haría - Famara (Walk 7)

- Historical Teguise (Walk 13)

HARÍA

Located in the north of Lanzarote, Haría is a municipal region that measures approximately 107 km² and stands 270 m above sea level. It is known as the 'Valley of a Thousand Palms' and is built on aquifer of the Famara cliff hence the presence of hundreds of wells used for drawing water.

of the San José chapel and farmstead. The other option is to carry on heading southwest until you reach the Teguise secondary school and the football pitch. Walk along *calle Gadifer de La Salle* street, *calle Villa* and *Puerto de Garachico* streets and you will reach *Plaza de la Mareta*. This is a wide open square built on top of Teguise's old *mareta* - the water storage reservoir once used by the former inhabitants of Lanzarote. Continue down *José Mann* and *Zonzamas* streets and you reach the *Plaza de La Constitución* square (220 m above sea level). You are now in the historical centre of Lanzarote's former capital, overlooked by the Nuestra Señora de Guadalupe church, the Palacio Spínola stately home and the ancient tithe barn, *la Cilla*. This beautiful square marks the end of this route.

Alternative route

Haría - Bosquecillo.
(See Arrieta - Haría - Famara walk)

Although Haría square is still your starting point, on this alternative route you should now head for the town hall. Walk along *La Longuera* street and turn left into *Ángel Guerra*, then turn right towards street *Barranco Malpaso*. Keep going along this road past the football pitch, the OAP Centre and the Luis Montero Canarian wrestling club. The street turns into a dirt road and then into a footpath that follows the ravine. After a long stretch following this ravine path you will come across examples of some endemic plants such as the Famara daisy (*Argyrathemun maderense*), Arabian peas (*Bituminaria bituminosa*), the fennel-like *tajasnoyos* (*Ferula lancerottensis*), the endemic verode succulent (*Aeonium lancerottense*), or some other indigenous plants such as the cliff dwelling thistle (*Sonchus pinnatifidus*) and fennel (*Foeniculum vulgare*). You will also see plants that have been introduced on the island such as the agave (*Agave americana*) and the henequen (*Agave fourcroydes*) or trees like the red-eyed wattle (*Acacia cyclops*). Stone steps

POINTS OF INTEREST

The Ermita de San José Chapel and Farmstead Ruins

These ruins date back to the 17th century and stand in the plain of the same name. The San José plain was once a hugely important area as the fertile soil made it excellent agricultural land. Today we can see huge hollows caused by the sale of this clay-like soil for use in crop fields on other parts of the island. At one time a chapel stood proudly in the grounds of the farmstead. It was a place of worship that was a compulsory stop-off point when pilgrims would descend from the mountain-top sanctuary bearing the statue of the Virgin of Las Nieves en route for Teguise. Many faithful pilgrims came here from all over the island carrying statues of San Sebastián from El Mojón, San Leandro from Teseguite and on occasion, even Saint Rafael and Christ on the cross would have been carried from Teguise itself.

POINTS OF INTEREST

The Iglesia de la Encarnación and Iglesia de San Juan churches in Haría

The ancient Encarnación church dates back to 1619 and even predates the creation of the parish which was established in 1631. However, it is not the oldest church in Haría asthat status belongs to the San Juan Bautista church which was built in the16th century. The church that stands today is actually a 20th century building, as it had to be rebuilt after torrential wind and rains battered down the original church on 22nd February 1956. The bell and the clock were donated by locals at the beginning of the 20th century.

The Ermita de Las Nieves Chapel

Some sources make reference to this chapel as far back as the 16th century but it was not until the 17th century that it is clearly named in records. It is impossible to put an exact date to when it was built as many historical documents were lost or destroyed during the numerous pirate attacks, raids and fires that Teguise suffered in the past.

The celebration that honours this Virgin falls on 5th August when the faithful from the surrounding villages make their way to the chapel in religious pilgrimage. They used to parade the statue of the Virgin down to Teguise, especially in times of drought. Later, in the 19th century and early 20th century it was established that this would take place every five years, and more often if there was drought. The last time the statue was carried down to Teguise was at the end of the Spanish Civil War in 1939.

The building that now stands was restored in the 1960s as the chapel was in virtual ruins. Devotion to the Virgin of Las Nieves is still very much in the hearts and minds of the people of Teguise, its neighbouring villages and the rest of the island.

indicate where this track comes to an end and turns into a dirt road. On the left you will see a slope covered with lots of unusual plants, some of which are local, like the endemic Famara convolvulus (*Conovolvulus lopezsocasi*) and the *Tajosé* thyme (*Thymus origanoides*). This path continues along the trail opposite which takes you towards the head of the ravine. Once you reach the reforested pine grove (*Pinus canariensis and Pinus halepensis*) the path takes you left and starts to ascend in a zigzag eventually heading south. The pine grove is an ideal place to stop and watch and listen to the birds. You are likely to see and hear canaries (*Serinus canaria*), European goldfinch (*Carduelis carduelis*), African blue tits (*Cyanistes terneriffae*), rock pigeons (*Columbia livia*), kestrels (*Falco tinnunculus*), southern grey shrikes (*Lanius meridionalis*) and Berthelot's pipits (*Anthus berthelotii*), to name a few. When the ravine ends, follow the narrower track between farm walls heading south until you reach the *Bosquecillo* forest; it is a recreational area which has been reforested with red-eyed wattle trees (*Acacia cyclops*) and Canary wild olive trees (*Olea cerasiformis*).

The views from this vantage point are truly breathtaking. From the children's play area you can follow the dirt track east until reaching the asphalt path and then turn right heading south. The path here is asphalted and heads to the Las Nieves chapel and back to the Haría-Teguise walk.

Walk 3

Lanzarote from north to south: Teguise - Tías

Difficulty rating: moderate
Type: linear
Approximate distance: 15 kilometres
Approximate timing: 4 hours
Terrain elevation: 300 361

Signposting: only one section marked route GR131 with white and red stripes

Departure point: Plaza de la Constitución square
UTM: 28 R6401763215411
Finishing point: Iglesia de la Candelaria church
UTM: 28 R6317943204994

Suitable for families with children and users of joëlettes or specially adapted wheelchairs.

The departure point for this trail is Teguise - a historical town that seems frozen in time as you wander around its cobbled streets, old churches, town square, stately homes and palaces which are now museums. When leaving Teguise behind you, this walk takes you across a sea of coarse white sand known as *jable* which separates Teguise from San Bartolomé. This *jable* sand creates a fertile desert which, thanks to their Herculean efforts, locals have managed to farm; cultivating produce such as sweet potatoes, watermelons and melons. The walk then takes you across San Bartolomé from tip to tip; a town that also boasts an important rural history and where a few traditional industries such as *gofio* production still endure. This trek also takes in Montaña Blanca, a small hamlet which lies at the foot of the mountain of the same name with its picturesque white-washed houses surrounded by fields of black volcanic pebbles. The finishing point is Tías, one of the island's largest towns in the south.

Casa Mayor Guerra manor house.

Walk 3

Walk description

From the *Plaza de La Constitución* square in Teguise which is steeped in history, you need to find *calle León y Castillo* and then *José Betancor* streets that lead you out of town heading southwest. When you have passed the petrol station, take the left-hand asphalt road that runs past Teguise's new cemetery. Keep walking until you get to the LZ-408 road, cross it and head south walking through the white *jable* fields formed by organogenic sand that has been blown in from Famara.

On the right you can see a volcanic rock quarry which was originally part of the lava flow from the Timanfaya volcanoes, specifically the *Volcán de las Nueces* volcano. Keep heading southwest ignoring the left-hand fork and sticking to the main path to San Bartolomé. You will see more paths that go off to the left and right but ignore those too and

HOW TO GET THERE

By bus: there are regular public transport links between Arrecife and Teguise.
By road: from Arrecife along the LZ-1 and LZ-10

POINTS OF INTEREST

- A brief history of Teguise
- A brief history of San Bartolomé (continued overleaf)

- The history of the barilla saltwort plant
- The Guatisea Maretas water reservoirs.
- The Montaña Blanca water reservoirs
- The Montaña Blanca and Guatisea Archaeological sites
- The Montaña Blanca cheesemakers
- Sweet potato cultivation
- Historical city of Teguise and surrounding areas with lime ovens, the San Rafael chapel and Santa Bárbara Castle. See Walk 13 - Historical Teguise.

keep to the trail that goes gently uphill between sweet potato fields planted in *jable* fields. As you continue, you will approach some rocky outcrops that jut out above the flat sandy fields. After walking a little further southwest, you will see the town of San Bartolomé ahead of you. Enter via *calle Rubicón* which crosses the town and takes you right out the other side towards Montaña Blanca.

Once you are in San Bartolomé, a stopover at the Tanit Museum is highly recommended. A visit to the *León y Castillo* plaza is also worthwhile where you can see the church and the local theatre and town hall. Continue heading down *calle Rubicón* street and you will pass an old windmill in ruins which dates back to the turn of the 20th century and belonged to Juan Armas. To the left stands the José María Gil windmill constructed at the end of the 19th century. It is still a working windmill and if you pass at the right time, you will be able to see and smell the grinding and roasting of the cereals such as wheat and corn, producing *gofio*, which used to be part of the islanders' staple diet.

As you leave San Bartolomé, still on *calle Rubicón* street, you will see the Casa Mayor Guerra manor house which was built in the 18th

San Bartolomé church.

Walk 3

ROUTE PROFILE

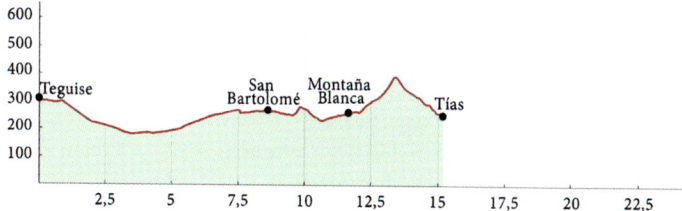

century and belonged to Francisco Tomás Guerra y Clavijo, known as 'Mayor Guerra'. He was a military man with great economic and political influence who lived at the end of the 18th century and the beginning of the 19th century. He helped fund the building of San Bartolomé's church at the end of the 18th century and its Los Dolores chapel is the final resting place for both he and his wife.

Keeping to the verge on the right, walk 50 metres south, parallel to *calle Rubicón* which turns into the LZ-35 main road to Montaña Blanca and Tías. There are two trails off to the right; one takes you to the Casa Mayor Guerra manor house and the second one heads southwest. This is the dirt track you should take to Mount Guatisea. After a few twists and turns, but still heading southwest, you come to a crossroads where you need to take the left turn, south. You will then start to walk along the foot of Mount Guatisea along *San Bartolomé* street. Just before you enter Montaña Blanca, there is a trail on the right which you could take if you want to see the Guatisea *Maretas* - a work of hydraulic engineering that was built in the 20th century to collect the run-off water from the mountain and channel it to the six water deposits excavated inside the mountain. Back on the trail that takes you into Montaña Blanca, cross the LZ-301, walk up *Lomo de Tesa* street and if you wish you can follow it uphill where you will find the María Auxiliadora church (1952) at the end, together with the local social club and school. This road turns into *La Degollada* street which then becomes a track as it leads out of the

LINKS WITH OTHER WALKS

- Montaña Blanca (Walk 14)

- Puerto del Carmen - Tinajo - La Santa (Walk 6)

village. If you choose *El Especiero* street, you can then follow the Montaña Blanca ravine which climbs up to the Las Vistas summit point which joins La Degollada path. Halfway along this path on the left-hand side, you will see the ascent up to the top of Montaña Blanca, standind proudly at 598m, and which rewards you with stunning views of nearly all the island (see Walk 14).

From the Las Vistas summit point, you can see Tías and the southern coast of Lanzarote, the islet of Los Lobos, and the island of Fuerteventura. Take your time to enjoy the superb views and then you can start to make the descent down heading south. On the way you will see the top of the bell tower of the 18th century La Candelaria church. Keep heading south and you will reach the end of the route in the town of Tías, but the town centre is still a fair distance away. Be careful as you come down *La Candelaria* street as it turns into the LZ-35 main road which eventually takes you into the central avenue of Tías just after the hardware store on the corner.

Alternative route

An alternative route is to climb Montaña de la Cruz behind the Casa Mayor Guerra manor house and after skirting around *Caldera Honda* and *Caldera Llana* calderas, you can enter the Guatisea crater following the GR-131 hiking trail signs.

TÍAS

- The **La Candelaria church** was built at the end of the 18th century and is the final resting place for some of the residents whose towns were engulfed by the volcanic eruptions. Located next to is the old cemetery.

- The **Ermita de San Antonio chapel** was built at the beginning of the 19th century and now houses an art gallery.

La Candelaria church.

POINTS OF INTEREST

A brief history of Teguise

At the beginning of the fifteenth century the Spanish conquistadors re-christened the indigenous town of Acatife and called it the city of Teguise. It became the island's capital and remained as such until 1852 when it lost its status as capital to Arrecife, after the so-called *Guerra Chica*, or 'small war'. Teguise was a city-state from which the lords of the island exercised their power over the inhabitants; the first to govern were the Bethencourts and then came the Herreras. Today we can wander around its streets and alleys and visit ancient palaces, monasteries, churches, archives and libraries etc. Teguise has the stately air of a bygone era - walking through its streets is akin to walking back in time into centuries past. (Walk 13)

A brief history of San Bartolomé

The town of San Bartolomé is situated right in the centre of Lanzarote. Its origins date back to the times of the pre-conquest when it was called Ajei. There are important archaeological sites in Montaña Guatisea and in Montaña Mina mountains where a collective human burial site was discovered in one of its caves.

By the end of the 18th century, San Bartolomé had a sizeable population and a parish of its own. At the beginning of the 19th century it won independence from Teguise, becoming a separate municipality in its own right.

Sweet Potato cultivation

The sweet potato (*Ipomoea batatas*) was the main crop grown in the *jable* fields throughout most of the 20th century with crop yields of more than 5,000.000 kilos per year which were exported to England, Holland, the rest of the Canary Islands and also the west coast of Africa. In 1970 there were 1,323 hectares of *jable* fields dedicated to sweet potato cultivation; today a mere 200 hectares remain. Sweet potato farming was such a major part of local life in San Bartolomé that local inhabitants are nicknamed *batateros* from the Spanish word for sweet potato; *batata*. Together with salted fish, the sweet potato forms part of one of Lanzarote's most unique local dishes called *sancocho*.

History of barrilla saltwort or common ice plant

According to legend, the priest José García Durán returned from captivity in Africa and started to cultivate the *barrilla* saltwort plant (*Mesembryanthemum crystallinum*) in the *jable* fields as long ago as in 1740. It was used to make soaps and its popularity was quick to catch on. Soon cultivation increased and it became the main crop on the island and was central to overseas trade. In 1798, 43,000 hundred weights of barrilla were exported, a figure which rose to 100,000 by 1808. It became such a successful crop that the majority of the island was farmed specifically for barrilla, but in so doing, vast quantities of indigenous plants such as the Mediterranean saltwort (*Salsola vermiculata*) and the spiny barbed-wire bush (*Launaea arborenscens*) were uprooted and used to fuel the fires that would burn the barilla, causing drastic deforestation. This loss of vegetation in the Famara region meant that when the wind whipped up the *jable* sand there were no natural barriers to stop it from spreading. The sand created dunes and sand storms that covered the island as far as Playa Honda and Los Pocillos and actually buried villages such as Fiquineo, Tao, Mozaga and San Bartolomé, forcing them to relocate or be lost forever. In the 19th century, local priest Baltasar Perdomo wrote in great detail of the *jable* sand storms and the human and agricultural disaster of the period.

Archaeological Site at Montaña Blanca and Montaña Guatisea

The southern flanks of both mountains shield remains of the culture of the men and women known as the *Majos* who lived on the island long before its conquest by Europeans. Canals of different sizes have been discovered together with petroglyphs, cup marks, drawings of triangular shapes, with criss-cross patterns, even animal shapes and heads of Billy goats. Together they make an enigmatic collection of remains which have yet to be fully deciphered.

Cheesemakers in Montaña Blanca

There are two large cheese producers in the village of Montaña Blanca; both are family-run and have their own goat herds. The tradition of cheese-making has been handed down over the years and is an inheritance from the farming traditions of the ancient inhabitants, the *Majos*. The Montaña Blanca cheesemakers is located in *calle Las Rosas* street and the El Especiero is in the street of the same name.

Walk 4

Lanzarote north to south: Tías - Yaiza

Difficulty rating: moderate
Type: linear
Approximate distance:
13.5 kilometres
Approximate timing:
3 hours 30 minutes
Terrain elevation:
320 ▲ 400 ▲
Signposting: marked as route GR131 with white and red stripes. Parts of the route are also marked as 'PR' (short route) in white and yellow stripes.

Departure point: Plaza de la Candelaria square
UTM:
28 R6317943204994
Finishing point:
Yaiza church
UTM:
28 R6203033203323

This route passes through part of the Protected Landscape of La Geria, and walks you through villages nestled in the sea of lava fields and volcanic ash called *rofe* which was carried by the wind from the volcanoes that erupted in the 18th century.

Taking Tías as your departure point, you will walk through Conil, across the gully and village of Tegoyo and the small town of La Asomada. You will be able to view La Geria from up high then venture forth through the network of semi-circular pits shielding vines and then through Tinasoria and Tablero. The trail then takes you to Uga, home to the majority of camels on the island.

Finally you will reach the small town of Yaiza via a track which runs right through fields of petrified lava - with each step you are reminded of the volcanic eruptions that sculpted this remarkable landscape.

Walk 4

Walk description

The starting point for this trail is the La Candelaria church in Tías. It is the oldest church in the parish (1796) and stands high in the La Candelaria area, 250 m above sea level. This church and the cemetery form part of the old town of Tías which was created after the Timanfaya eruptions. You will need to take the road north behind the church and where the paved road ends, turn left and cross the *Los Fajardos* road. Follow the dirt road called *Peña del Asiento* which takes you to Conil; a small hamlet with views over the south coast of the island and Fuerteventura. As you enter the village, you will reach a fork; take the left turn and walk along the paved path then cross the LZ-501 road and keep heading west along *calle Camino del Callao II* street. After descending

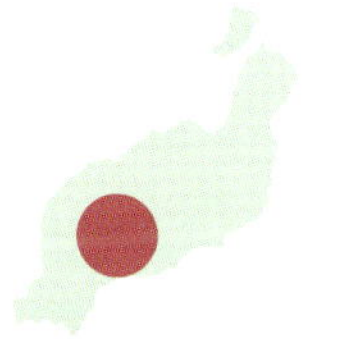

HOW TO GET THERE

By bus: there are regular public transport links between Arrecife and Tías.
By road: from Arrecife along the LZ-2

POINTS OF INTEREST

- Canarian wrestler Pollo de Uga (continued overleaf)

85

Tías - Yaiza

- Benito Pérez Armas Cultural Centre
- Camels in Lanzarote

POINTS OF INTEREST

In Tías:
see previous Walk.

In Tegoyo:
- **Ermita de Tegoyo chapel** (19th century)

In Uga:
Camel farms in **Vallito de Uga** valley

In Yaiza:
Nuestra Señora de los Remedios, 18th century church (see page 94)

Benito Pérez Armas Cultural Centre (see page 89)

for almost a kilometre, you will reach a group of houses in Tegoyo. Take the road west and you will see a no entry sign for vehicles except residents.

This trail continues after this sign and ascends westward towards La Asomada. It passes an *aljibe* water deposit and a big water catchment plain (*alcogida*) which looks like a sheet of concrete laid out at the foot of the Tegoyo hill (La Asomada mountain.) When this road comes to an end you will find you are at a stop sign next to a supermarket. Turn left and head south along the LZ-502 road, just a few metres along take either the first or the second on the right heading west. Both turnings take you to the *Camino de La Caldereta* path. Here in La Asomada on the LZ-502 you will find the local socio-cultural centre and the village church.

The *Camino de La Caldereta* path soon shakes off the asphalt and turns into a dirt road at the foot of Mount Guardilama, one of the highest peaks in Lanzarote (603 m.) The trail will take you up until you reach the top of Mount Tinasoria, if you look to the south you will see its crater is covered with vines planted beneath a layer of coarse black volcanic sand (*lapilli*). From the uppermost point of this Tinasoria path you can then make the descent,

Walk 4

ROUTE PROFILE

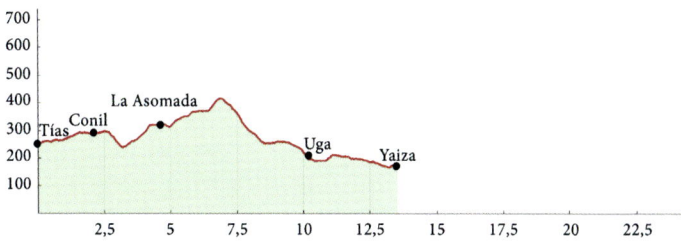

always heading in the same westerly direction and then southwest. The path then becomes the Tablero path. Keep walking among the vines planted beneath the volcanic ash ejected by the the 18th century volcanoes. Soon you will be in the region called La Geria, a fascinating landscape crafted by man. Local farmers dug deep pits in the volcanic ash to plant vines and fruit trees and then carefully constructed semi-circular stone walls to protect their crops from the continual assault of the trade winds.

Once you reach the La Geria LZ-30 road, turn left and head south for approximately 40 metres, turn right and take a dirt track downhill that takes you all the way to Uga.

Uga was another village affected by the volcanic eruptions in Timanfaya as its fertile plains and some of its houses were engulfed by the lava flow. When you reach *calle los Arenales* street, keep south and walk around a children's play park on the right. Then take the main street (*Joaquín Rodríguez*) named after Lanzarote's best Canarian wrestler who fought at the beginning of the 20th century and who made his home town of Uga famous throughout the Canary Islands.

Here you will find the modern church built in the 20th century in honour of the saint, San Isidro Labrador. Uga is a town with strong farming and agricultural traditions. Today it is home to the largest population of camels (as dromedaries are known on Lanzarote) on the island. They have survived the test of

LINKS WITH OTHER WALKS

- Montaña Blanca (Walk 14)

- Puerto del Carmen
- Tinajo - La Santa (Walk 6)

- La Geria (Walk 18)

An ecclectic-style house in the village of Uga.

time thanks to the fact that they have become a tourist attraction in their own right as they take visitors for rides in Timanfaya National Park.

When you reach the LZ-2 road, take a dirt road that turns right, northwest. On the left you will see the underground tunnel through which the camels pass to get back to their farms in Vallito de Uga where they have their well-earned rest after a hard day's work on the Fire Mountains. The dirt road continues northwest and then it becomes a footpath that heads west, crossing a lava field. Be careful along this path as you may well come across a caravan of camels either on their way to or back from Timanfaya. When you reach a crossroads in the path, walk under the bridge and enter Yaiza along *calle Montañas del Fuego* street. Yaiza is one of the most peaceful and best kept villages on the island with beautiful old buildings standing side by side with modern architecture. Go past the petrol

POINTS OF INTEREST

Pollo de Uga (1895-1959)

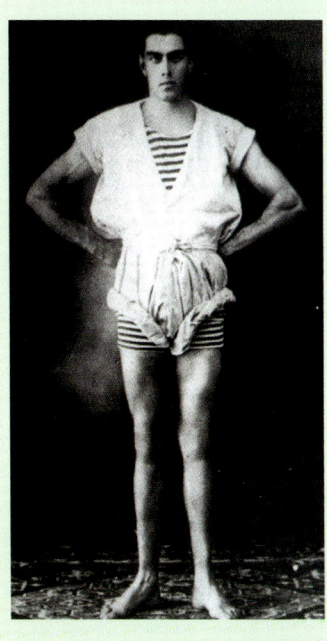

This was the nickname of Canarian wrestler Joaquín Rodríguez Cabrera who was in his prime at the beginning of the 20th century. The nickname "pollo", (chicken) is still given to any Canarian wrestler who shows outstanding abilities and strength from a young age. In the 1920s "Pollo de Uga" proudly made his hometown of Uga a well-known town throughout the Canarian archipelago. We can still read about tales of legendary bouts and duels in the newspaper archives with details of wrestling matches against many opponents including Pancho Suárez (Pollo de los Campitos) who he took on in the packed out bullring in Santa Cruz, Tenerife, Pedro Rodríguez (Pollo de Las Canteras) and Justo Mesa in Las Palmas in Gran Canaria. Nowadays, Uga maintains its wrestling tradition and still has its own club, Union Sur, Yaiza, which trains wrestlers for competition representing the municipal region of Yaiza.

Casa de la Cultura Benito Pérez Armas Cultural Centre (Yaiza)

This is a historical building that dates back to the 18th century situated in the Los Remedios plaza in Yaiza. It was the birthplace of writer, journalist and politician, Benito Pérez Armas. It is an example of traditional Canarian architecture. It was restored in 1990 and converted into the Yaiza town hall's cultural centre, or *Casa de Cultura*. Today, it hosts cultural activities such as exhibitions, poetry readings, concerts, plays and so forth. It also houses the municipal library and other departments belonging to the town hall.

Benito Pérez Armas was born in Yaiza in 1871 where he was brought up. He then moved to Las Palmas to study and went on to continue his studies in Salamanca and Seville. He returned to the Canaries and made Tenerife his home until he died in 1937. He was the director of magazines and newspapers and enjoyed posts in local government as chairman of the Canarian county council and Member of Parliament. He penned various novels; "La Baja del Secreto", "Las lágrimas de Camella", "Rosalba", "De padres a hijos", "Escenas marineras", "Recuerdos de la niñez y la juventud", "Tradiciones y anécdotas Canarias" and "Un viaje al Teide", to name but a few.

Camels in Lanzarote

The dromedary (*Camelus dromedarius*), popularly known as the 'camel', has been a part of Lanzarote life and has been working alongside islanders since the fifteenth century. Once the island was conquered, forced labour was brought over from neighbouring Africa. Together with the slaves, they brought camels as working animals for carrying heavy loads. From this time on, camels have been used to undertake the arduous work of farming the fields, ploughing, sowing seeds and carrying straw, earth and rocks. The work of camels played a key role in shaping the agricultural landscape as they helped to build farms and farmlands and then worked them. They were also used to grind grain by moving the heavy millstones in the flour mills, to thresh the straw and extract the grain. They were also used as taxis to transport the occasional visitor to the island.

The camel population used to number more than 2,000 in the eighteenth century, with more than 3,000 registered in the 1940 census. Their decline in numbers coincided with the arrival of motor vehicles and trucks. Then the real turning point came in the 1970s when the island's economy shifted and agriculture gave way to tourism. The majority of camels were sold and sent to the Sahara in the 1970s and 1980s.

1948 was a key year in the camels' fate, however, as local Yaiza resident Miguel Díaz started to use camels to take visitors for rides in the Fire Mountains and in so doing prevented their virtual elimination from the island. Slowly, the number of camel drivers began to increase in line with the rise in tourism and a new niche was created. Today the largest camel population is in the *Vallito de Uga* valley where 400 camels live and work every day up in Timanfaya National Park.

station and the Civil Guard police station to get to the high street (*calle Vista de Yaiza*) where you turn right and will see the back of Nuestra Señora de los Remedios church right in front of you. The church has rows of ombu trees around it (*Phytolaca dioica*) brought over by an emigrant from South America; these mark the end of this trail.

Alternative routes

Once on top of Mount Tinasoria there is a trail that can take you on a quick detour to the left. Follow it towards some ruins to discover a great spot to enjoy views over Tías and the coastline below. Another alternative is to turn right towards the La Geria trail (Walk 18) towards the Guardilama mountain in the north, but bear in mind that the steep climb makes it a tricky ascent.. Another alternative to the La Geria trail (Walk 18) is the one that takes you to the Ermita de La Caridad chapel and the Bodegas La Geria vineyards.

Walk 5
Lanzarote north to south: Yaiza - Playa Blanca

Difficulty rating: moderate
Type: linear
Approximate distance: 13.3 kilometres
Approximate timing: 3 hours 30 minutes
Terrain elevation: 121 345
Signposting: marked as route GR131 with white and red signs.

Departure point: Yaiza church
UTM: 28 R6203033203323
Finishing point: Yaiza church
UTM: 28 R6143993193401

This walk takes you from the village of Yaiza to the resort of Playa Blanca, and weaves across the dry, barren plains and rocky terrain that separate these two towns. Walkers are rewared with the perfect opportunity to marvel at the incredible scenery in the south, including the volcanoes in Timanfaya, the neighbouring island of Fuerteventura clearly visible on the horizon and the beaches on the south coast.

The walk takes you over the remains of the old *malpaís*, or 'badlands' of petrified lava fields produced by the *Atalaya de Femés* volcano, which at 609 m is the highest on the island. The village of Las Breñas marks the halfway point of the walk and is the perfect spot to look out at the vast area of rocky lowlands stretching before you and which need to be tackled before reaching Playa Blanca.

Walk 5

Walk description

Starting at the *Nuestra Señora de los Remedios* church in Yaiza, you will need to head off in a westerly direction along the main street, *Vista de Yaiza*. Continue along for 600 metres and then just before reaching the football pitch, take a left turn up some stone steps that to a dirt path that takes you up the reddish coloured gardens on this side of Yaiza. The view looking west is of a vast sea of petrified lava encircling orange-hued mountains that look almost as though trapped by the eruptions in the 18th century. Keep heading southwest like before, but now higher up. This route almost coincides with the old road that runs to Playa Blanca. On the left you will see a house with olive trees planted in terraces. When it seems as if the path comes to an end, follow the dirt track downhill on the left. When

HOW TO GET THERE

By bus: there are regular public transport links between Arrecife and Yaiza.
By road: from Arrecife along the LZ-2

POINTS OF INTEREST

- The Nuestra Señora de Los Remedios Church

93

Yaiza - Playa Blanca

PLACES TO VISIT

<u>In Yaiza:</u>
- The 18th century Nuestra Señora de los Remedios church
- The Casa Benito Pérez Armas house

<u>In Playa Blanca:</u>
- The Pechiguera lighthouse ("faro")

you have descended a few metres, do not take the first junction to the left, instead turn south on the second path which takes you to the village of Las Breñas. As you arrive you will find a stone path that opens up into the *La Cancela* street. Las Breñas is the ideal place to stop and get your strength back before continuing with the next stage of the walk.

There is a small chapel in honour of Saint Luis Gonzaga - patron saint of youth - and there is a plaza and a children's play park. Walk down

POINTS OF INTEREST

Nuestra Señora de los Remedios Church (18th century)

There is some dispute as to the exact age of this church. Some scholars argue that it dates back to the 17th century and others, the majority, in fact, state that it was built at the beginning of the 18th century in accordance with the date of 1699 stated in the construction archive.

Its sheer distance away from Teguise prompted residents in Yaiza to build a church. Years later, in 1728, it became a parish in its own right. The first parish priest was Andrés Lorenzo Curbelo and it was he who witnessed the first eruptions in Timanfaya and diarised the event back on 1st September 1730.

Walk 5

ROUTE PROFILE

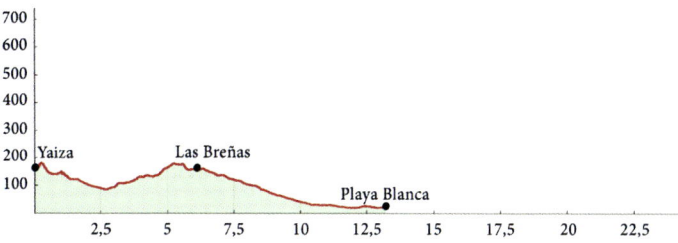

calle Víctor Fernández Gopar street, named after an illustrious personality of the town; he was overseer of the Janubio saltworks and also a great popular poet who would express his feelings through verse and texts that have been much published and cherished over the years. At the end of this road, turn into *Los Roques* street to leave the village heading south down a track with a goat farm on the left-hand side. Pass a small mound of basalt rock called Los Roques and take the first path on the right which heads south. You will find it rather sparse and lifeless with just the occasional barilla saltwort plant (*Salsola vermiculata*), spiny tea tree shrub (*Licium intricatum*) and a handful of barbed wire bushes (*Launaea arborescens*) for company.

A note of caution; this is a rocky path which can be uncomfortable underfoot, but it takes you straight to Playa Blanca. One solitary house stands near the end of the path and large volcanic ash-covered field. You then get to a dirt track and when you reach the intersection with another trail, take the left-hand fork and this takes you to *calle Rubicón* street. In this street you can take a right turn so that you can then take any of the three streets down to the sea (*calle Janubio / calle Hacha Grande / calle La Lapa*). You could also get to the seafront via the children's play park at the end of this street. Once on the *Avenida Papagayo* avenue, keep walking right and you will come to the Nuestra Señora del Carmen church in Playa Blanca and you have reached the end of this walk.

LINKS TO OTHER WALKS

- Papagayo (Walk 20)

- Playa Blanca - Janubio (Walk 9)

95

Walk 6: Puerto del Carmen - Tinajo - La Santa

Difficulty rating: moderate
Type: linear
Approximate distance: 28 kilometres
Approximate timing: 7 hours
Terrain gradient: 607 ▲ 607 ▲
Signposting: some small 'PR' trails marked yellow and white and some marked as SL, or local trails which are white and green stripes.

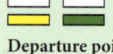

Departure point: Puerto del Carmen
UTM: 28 R6334973200934
Finishing point: La Santa
UTM: 28 R6298293220818

This route takes you right across the heart of Lanzarote from the east to the west coast over the widest part of the island. This walk particularly stands out for its wide variety of landscapes and scenery including coastal landscapes, tourist areas, volcanoes, farmlands - all of which have played an important role in the island's history and development over the centuries. You will be able to see Puerto del Carmen, Tías, Montaña Blanca, El Grifo, La Cueva de los Naturalistas (Las Palomas), Las Quemadas, the Los Dolores church, Tinajo, La Cueva de Ana Viciosa cave and La Santa.

It is a walk that encompasses areas of great cultural and historical importance which reveal the quintessential feel of the island's history and nature.

Walk 6

Walk description

Puerto del Carmen - Tías - Montaña Blanca

Standing on the Puerto del Carmen coast at the Los Pocillos beach, locate the roundabout where the beachfront avenue crosses with *calle Marte* street. Take the alley north that runs parallel with the channelled ravine that marks the end of the los Pocillos gully. Once in *calle Júpiter* street, take the dirt road which heads north in the direction of Tías. Walk along the middle of this open ravine and then go under the flyover with the main Puerto del Carmen ring road above (LZ-40) to head north, ignoring any forks. The path eventually twists right with an asphalted section called *Camino Mojón Negro*, which you need to keep to. You will then come to

HOW TO GET THERE

By bus: there are regular public transport links between Arrecife and Puerto del Carmen. By road: from Arrecife along the LZ-2 dual carriageway and then the LZ-40 road.

POINTS OF INTEREST

- La Candelaria church in Tías (continued overleaf)

97

Puerto del Carmen - Tinajo - La Santa

- Archaeological site in Montaña Blanca
- The los Naturalistas cave

PLACES OF INTEREST

- The los Dolores church
- The El Grifo winery
- The San Roque church
- The Ana Viciosa cave
- The La Santa salt marsh

an intersection of asphalted roads in the town of Tías where you take the first turning on the left and then turn to the right once more.

You should now be heading north and pass underneath the main LZ-2 road. You will then come into the *Barranco de las Truchas* road which you should follow westwards right until the end when it comes to the LZ-35. If you don't want to keep to the path heading north, take the left-hand turning here at the LZ-35 until you get to the roundabout next to the *Seño Justo* house which was converted into a Wine and farming Museum *Museo Agrícola y Enológico* but has since closed down. Take the right turn along *calle Candelaria* street heading northeast and you will get to the La Candelaria church which dates back to the 18th century. Here you need to take the road behind the church and go northwards

POINTS OF INTEREST

The Bodega El Grifo winery

The El Grifo winery stands at the point where the petrified lava flow meets the volcanic ash. The iconic griffin (*el grifo*) perches atop the gates and welcomes visitors to this oldest winery on the island, founded in 1775. Given that the period of volcanic eruptions came to an end in approximately 1735, it is clear that the island's farmers were quick to invent their ingenious method of growing grapes, as it was only 40 years later that they started to produce wines and liqueurs. This family-run winery, or *bodega*, has long been, and still is, at the forefront of wine production and is renowned for its excellent malvasia wines. Part of the old buildings now houses the Museo del Vino wine museum which invites visitors to learn about the history of the winery and the unique method of grape-growing on the island.

Walk 6

ROUTE PROFILE

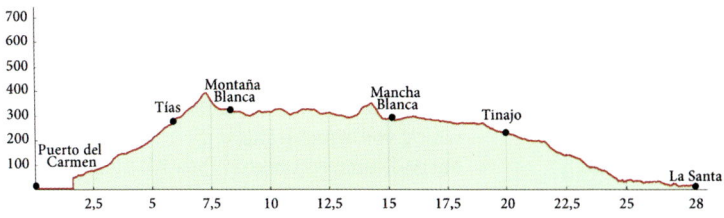

which first twists right along a dirt road and then left and then ascends, passing an open *aljibe* water deposit (*aljibe del Teniente*). After this, take the path that runs to the right which takes you to the narrow gorge which separates Montaña Blanca to your right from the Lomo de Tesa slope on your left. Once you have finished the ascent you can look down onto the village of Montaña Blanca below and you can start climbing down along the *La Degollada* path. Before you get to the first houses, take a left turning called the *Camino de los Cojos*.

LINKS WITH OTHER WALKS

- Montaña Blanca (Walk 14)

- Teguise - Tías (Walk 3)

- Caldera Blanca (Walk 15)

Montaña Blanca - Los Dolores church

When you come to the end of the *camino de los Cojos* lane you will reach an intersection with the LZ-301 which you should cross with caution and continue straight on, heading north along *calle Lagar* or *camino de las Cuevas* path. Take the bend left along the first dirt track and you will see a large gate with a no entry sign, keep walking along the footpath to the right which runs through vineyards. You will then reach another path; first turn left, then right along a footpath that takes you through a change in scenery; from seeing vines growing in round pits to vines growing in more rectangular-shaped ditches. Keep heading north up to the LZ-30 road where you will be greeted by a giant mythological griffin that stands guard at the El Grifo winery. The griffin was designed by César Manrique and is the *bodega's* logo. When you cross the road, you will see the *bodega* itself; it is the oldest in the Canary Islands. You can stop off and learn more about its history at the winemaking museum here, the *Museo del Vino*. From the entrance to the winery, head west, taking the first path right that you come across. You will now be walking through vines planted beneath the blanket of volcanic sand.

When you reach a junction, take the left-hand path (if you take the right-hand path it will lead you to the Los Bermejos winery.)Then head west along the way-marked path of a local trail. When you reach the northern face of the Juan Bello Mountain to your left you will see an old water collection plate and a water deposit where you should turn right and head north. You will then reach some fields of lava flow from the Timanfaya eruptions, specifically the *Volcán de Nueces* volcano which completely filled a huge ravine which once cleaved through the eastern part of the island. Walk along the *carretera del Peñón* road (LZ-58) northwards and 25 metres further on you will see the *Naturalistas* cave, or the *Las Palomas* cave as it is also known. It is an extensive volcanic tube with spectacular interior caverns. Keep walking along this road and then just before getting to a sharp gradient, turn left where a dirt road indicates the path to the rural hotel called Finca Tisalaya. Before getting to the hotel itself, turn right and take the trail that climbs up to the *El Alto*. Once you have reached the top, it is well worth pausing for a moment to admire the stunning scenery.

Walk down through the vine plantations called Las Quemadas and at a fork with palm trees, take the left-hand turn west. Keep on this main path all the way until you reach the LZ -46, then turn left to the Nuestra Señora de los Dolores chapel in Mancha Blanca. She is the patroness of the island with the saint's day celebration in her honour taking place on 15th September. It is an important religious and traditional festival for islanders, in which they undertake a pilgrimage to the church, bearing

The San Roque Church

The existence of a chapel in Tinajo in honour of San Roque dates back to the mid sixteenth century. It has undergone many extensions and refurbishments over the years that have shaped its current design.

Nuestra Señora de Los Dolores Church (Our Lady of Sorrows Church)

This is Lanzarote's most important shrine and it is where the statue of the patroness of the island, the Virgen de Los Dolores is kept. The chapel was built in 1781 in order to fulfil a promise made by the people of Tinajo in gratitude for that fateful day back in 1735 when they paraded out of the San Roque church carrying a statue of the Virgen de Los Dolores to confront the lava flow emanating from Montaña Colorada. According to legend, the lava flow came to a miraculous halt and subsequently the promise was made to build a church in honour of their patroness. A few years later, in 1774, a young local girl called Juana Rafaela, was herding her goats on Mount Guigan when the Virgin appeared before her and gave her a message to remind everyone about the unfulfilled promise to build the shrine.

The Virgen de Los Dolores also played a key role in the last eruption on the island which took place on 31st July 1824. Her statue was carried to Tao at the very mouth of the volcanic eruptions in the hope that she could intervene. These eruptions turned out to be far less effusive than previous ones and they stopped after just a few months, thus increasing devotion to the Virgin.

Photograph by Teodoro Maisch taken in 1928 provided by the Lanzarote Cabildo's Historical Heritage Service.

Puerto del Carmen - Tinajo - La Santa

The coastal hamlet of La Laja del Sol.

WHAT TO VISIT

Wine Museum - El Grifo
Open from 10.30 am - 6pm every day (including public holidays)

Book in advance for a guided tour around the museum and the vineyards including wine tasting. Monday to Sunday at 11.00am, 1pm, 4pm and 5pm Price: 4€ per person. Telephone: (+34 928 524 951)

- **Los Naturalistas Cave (a.k.a Las Palomas Cave)**

- **Los Dolores Church**

offerings to the saint. The festival is well-known for its craft fair and its folk singing and dancing celebrations.

Los Dolores church - Tinajo - La Santa

With the entrance to the church behind you, take *calle Guiguan* street that leads to the village of Tinajo. At the first junction turn right along the *Avenida de los Volcanes* avenue which goes right through Tinajo. When you get to the town hall and the church you will find you are now in the town's main square. Make sure you stop to look at the sundial on the roof of the San Roque church. It was a gift from a local seaman from La Vegueta (a hamlet in the municipality of Tinajo) in 1851. The sundial registers the local sun hour and not the administrative time that we have on our watches and clocks. From this plaza, take *Juan Betancor* street or *Alcaraván* street just behind the church and follow the road northwest, this road turns into *calle Molino del Viento* street and when you are almost at the outskirts of the town, take the *Laja del Sol* street to the left. This asphalt road ends and becomes a dirt road which you will need to follow in a north-westerly direction at first and then north until you reach an intersection. The first trail to the right takes you straight to the village of La Santa, whilst the second trail north takes you down to the small coastal hamlet of Laja del Sol. An interesting detour is to take this path

Ana Viciosa Cave

This cave is steeped in legend and is situated in the Los Cuchillos cliffs next to the coastal hamlet of La Laja del Sol. Access is difficult and it is walled with rocks and limestone. It is named after Ana Viciosa a lady from Mount Clara. She was the wife of Juan de León Muxia, governor of Lanzarote and owner of the feudal state of Tíngafa (now known as Tinajo). The lord died young in the middle of the 17th century and bequeathed his wife all his lands. Her power, position and widowhood generated all sorts of tales of love affairs with slaves and young farmhands of the district with these amorous escapades allegedly taking place in the cave; there were even tales of her dalliance with Dog Head the Pirate - although it has to said to be said that he was around in the 19th century, so he would not actually have been a peer!

Los Naturalistas Cave

The Naturalistas Cave is also known as the Palomas cave and is a short volcanic tube with enormous caverns that are quite spectacular to behold. It was created by the eruption of the Nueces volcano in the 18th century. The lava spill gushed out towards the east and completely filled one of the island's biggest ravines. The sea of lava went through Tomaren, Mozaga and the area where the agricultural industrial park of Teguise now stands before forking off in two directions; one part went down to Famara, the other headed for Tahíche and Arrecife. This cave is remarkable because of the sheer size of its caverns. It has numerous stalactites hanging down from the roof of the cave and a fairly flat floor which makes it easy to explore, but care is needed in some areas where there is loose scree underfoot. This volcanic tube is a Natural Monument and is protected by Decree-Law 1/2000 that governs Protected Spaces in the Canaries.

Puerto del Carmen - Tinajo - La Santa

The small harbour at La Santa.

and walk down to the houses in this hamlet and then take a left turn under the cliff until you reach the Ana Viciosa cave. It is barely visible and rather impregnable, seemingly suspended in the middle of the cliff face. You will need to look carefully to make out the entrance covered by a small wall of rocks and limestone and a small doorway in an opening that serves as a window, or look-out point. This cave has been mentioned in numerous popular myths and legends about Ana Viciosa, one of the biggest landowners of the Tingafa-Tinajo region.

From up high in Laja del Sol, you can take the coastal footpath northeast that takes you to Montaña Bermeja. Take the path northeast now to Los Picachos, which is just before you arrive in La Santa along the *Las Betancoras* road.

La Santa is a small village on the northern coast of Tinajo which still thrives on fishing and whose prized La Santa prawn is highly sought after. It also enjoys tourist income thanks to its bars and restaurants and the Club La Santa sports centre which has been providing accommodation and superb facilities to elite sports men and women from all over Europe for over thirty years. It is also the organisation behind the world-renowned Ironman triathlon. The area between the village of La Santa and the Club La Santa sports resort is also an area of ecological interest as it is home to the island's unique salt marsh. It is an area which floods at high tide and which is laid bare, exposed to the sun at low tide and is subsequently home to a remarkable variety of endemic flora and fauna.

Walk 6

The La Santa salt marsh

Lying between the village of La Santa and Club La Santa is the salt marsh (*saladar*). It is a unique ecosystem as the animals and plants that live there can survive the invasion of the sea at high tide and exposure to the harsh sun at low tide. It is home to many waders such as the common ringed plover (*Charadrius hiaticula*), the Kentish plover (*Charadrius alexandrius)*, the whimbrel (*Numenius phaeopus*), the common greenshank (*Tringa nebularia*), the ruddy turnstone (*Arenaria interpres*), the little egret (*Egretta garzetta*), the Eurasian spoonbill (*Platalea leucorodia*), the grey plover (*Pluviales squatarola*), the common redshank (*Tringa totanus*), the common sandpiper (*Actitis hypoleucos*), to name but a few. It is an ideal spot for lovers of birding; it is always advisable to maintain good distance so as not to disturb the birds and in this way you will be able to enjoy observing many different species.

The salt marsh is also home to many different plants, some of which are completely unique to this area, including; glasswort (*Arthrocnemun fructicosum*), chicken claws (*Sarcocornia perennis*), the Canary sea fennel (*Astydamia latifolia*), the shrubby sea-blite (*Suaeda vera*) and the *Tetraena fontanesii* bunge.

Walk 7 — Arrieta - Haría - Famara

Difficulty rating: moderate
Type: linear
Approximate distance: 16 kilometres
Approximate timing: 5 hours 30 minutes
Terrain gradient: 638 / 647
Signposting: only some small 'PR' trails marked yellow and white and some marked as 'SL', or local trails which are white and green.

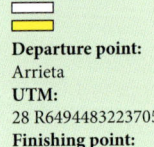

Departure point: Arrieta
UTM: 28 R6494483223705
Finishing point: Caleta de Famara
UTM: 28 R6396903221811

This walking trail connects two uniquely special beaches; the La Garita in Arrieta (Haría) and Famara beach (Teguise). The walk both begins and ends at sea level and takes you across Lanzarote from east to west, over the narrowest part of the island.

The trails starts off with an ascent through Haría; one of the island's most picturesque villages with its palm trees and traditional old whitewashed houses. It then leads you up to the little forest, locally known as the Bosquecillo which stands at this trail's highest point above sea level on the side of the Famara cliff which is the real star of this walk. From the Bosquecillo you will start a spectacular descent down the Poceta ravine also named the 'Rincón de la Paja' where the stunning landscape brings you down to Famara, the longest beach on the island.

Walk 7

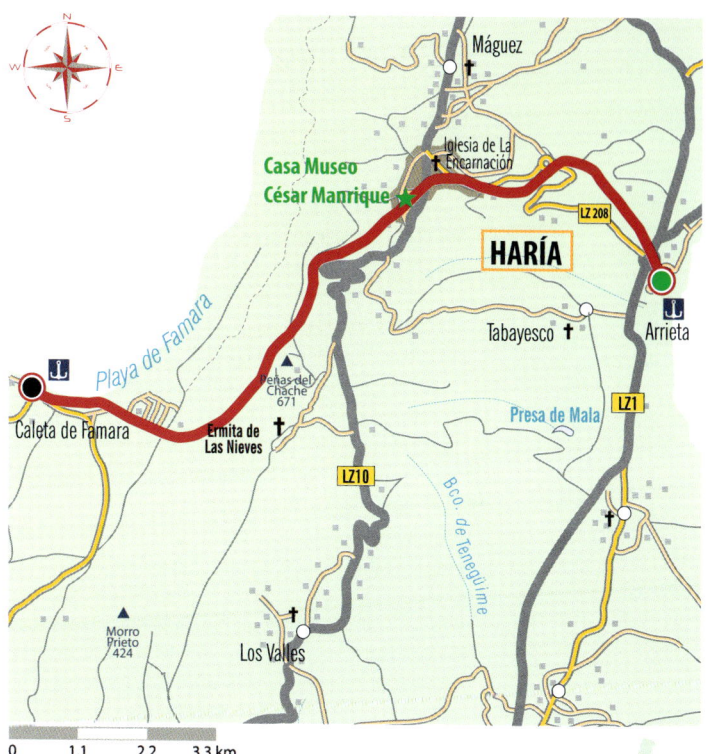

Walk description

Arrieta - Haría

Standing on *calle Arcoiris* street, head towards the roundabout at the entrance to Arrieta with its eye-catching wind sculpture designed by César Manrique. The trail goes northwards along a dirt road alongside a gully and then opens out into a wider ravine that takes you north past electricity cables held up by posts and then eventually on to the water purifying station. Still heading north, start the ascent up a zig-zag dirt path; using the antennae at the top as a landmark to guide you. Once you have finished the climb you have the choice between following the Barranco de Tenesía ravine or taking the trail that bears left. Taking this trail leads you to the LZ-208 road which you need to cross. You will now be on an

HOW TO GET THERE

By bus: there are regular public transport links between Arrecife and Arrieta.
By road: from Arrecife along the LZ-1

POINTS OF INTEREST

The Encarnación Church
(continued overleaf)

Arrieta - Haría - Famara

- The *Bosquecillo* little forest
- The Famara spring and water tunnels
- Famara cove
- The Archipelago Chinijo Natural Park

CYNEGETIC SPECIES

Barbary partridge
(*Alectoris barbara*)

European Rabbit
(*Oryctolagus cuniculus*)

asphalted road called *Cuesta del Pozo* next to the local police station. Then join the San Juan road where you'll see the church is of the same name, (page 74). If you follow this road, you will pass the bronze sculpture in honour of, the now deceased Canarian wrestler, Tony Martín or 'Pollo del Puerto', as he was nicknamed. A few metres ahead you will see the back of the Encarnación church which takes you to Haría's main square.

Haría - Bosquecillo

From Haría's main square you need to head for the town hall and walk along *calle La Longuera* and then take the left turning into *calle Ángel Guerra* street towards *calle Barranco Malpaso* street, walking past the Ladislao Rodríguez Bonilla football pitch and the centre for the elderly. The road turns into a dirt road and then a trail that follows the course of the dried-up river bed. After a long stretch you will start to see an array of endemic species like the Famara daisy (*Argyranthemun maderense*), the fennel-like *tajasnoyos* (*Ferula lancerottensis*), the endemic verode succulent (*Aeonium lancerottense*), and other native vegetation such as the cliff dwelling thistle (*Sonchus pinnatifidus*) or Arabian pea (*Bituminaria bituminosa*). There are also plants of more widespread distribution like the hardy fennel (*Foeniculum vulgare*) and species that have been introduced by man, such as the agave (*Agave americana*) and the henequen (*Agave fourcroydes*) or trees like the red-eyed wattle (*Acacia cyclops*). At the end of this ravine trail you can see a series of stone

The vantage point at the Bosquecillo forest.

ROUTE PROFILE

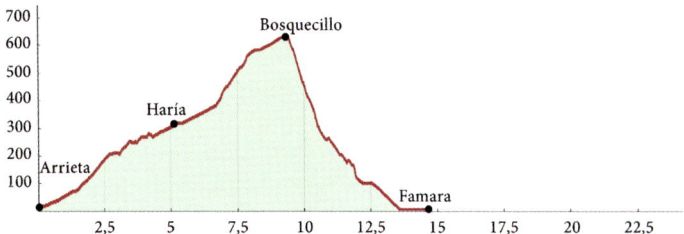

steps that lead to a dirt road. On the left you will see a slope covered with lots of rare plants, some of which are unique to the region like the Famara morning glory (*Conovolvulus lopezsocasi*) and the *Tajosé* thyme (*Thymus origanoides*). Continue along the footpath opposite which takes you towards the head of the ravine. Once you reach the reforested pine grove, populated with the Canary pine tree (*Pinus canariensis*) and the aleppo pine (*Pinus halepensis*), the path bends to the left and starts to ascend in a zigzag eventually heading south. The pine grove is an ideal place to stop and watch and listen to birds. You are likely to see and hear Atlantic canaries (*Serinus canaria*), European goldfinch (*Carduelis carduelis*), African blue tits (*Cyanistes terneriffae*), rock pigeons (*Columbia livia*), kestrels (*Falco tinnunculus*), southern grey shrikes (*Lanius meridionalis*), Berthelot's pipit (*Anthus berthelotii*) and many more. When the ravine ends, follow the narrower footpath between farm walls heading south until you reach the *Bosquecillo* forest; it is a recreational area which has been reforested with red-eyed wattle trees (Acacia cyclops) and Canary wild olive trees (Olea cerasiformis). This is a good moment to stop and properly take in the breathtaking views from the top of the cliff over the Chinijo archipelago which lies to the north and the sandy *jable* lowlands to the south.

LINKS TO OTHER ROUTES

- Haría - Teguise (Walk 2)

- Órzola - Haría (Walk 1)

Bosquecillo - Famara

Once at the vantage point in the *Bosquecillo* forest, locate the children's park and follow the footpath that runs near to the Famara cliff until you find a dirt road about 100 metres further on

Arrieta - Haría - Famara

CALETA DE FAMARA COVE

Is a natural cove whose residents have historically relied on fishing activities and shell fishing for sustenance. It was permanently inhabited from the 19th century on and it has also been the traditional summer vacation spot for many islanders, including César Manrique at one time. It is a popular village for residents and visitors alike and is the island's Mecca for aficionados of surfing and kite surfing.

to your left. Follow this and it will take you to another path to the right towards the head of the Poceta, (La Paja) ravine. The path that that takes you down the cliff is about 25 metres on your left. Take care as you descend as the path can be quite slippery in places. This trail snakes between balsamiferous spurge (*Euphorbia balsamifera*) and cliff dwelling thistles (*Sonchus pinnatifidus*). Halfway down, the footpath turns into a dirt road which makes the descent a little more comfortable from this point on. At the end of the ravine you will pass a house surrounded by a lot of vegetation and this is where you will find one of Famara's water galleries. These galleries were dug out at the beginning of the twentieth century to boost the volume of water collected at the source of the La Poceta spring. Next to this house also lie the foundations of the Las Mercedes hermitage built by the Franciscans in the fifteenth century but which had fallen into total disrepair by the 18th century. Keep going and you will reach the residential area known as Island Homes which is a collection of bungalows also referred to as 'the Norwegians'. After walking down the road that runs alongside them, you will be greeted by the sight of Famara beach whose stunning golden sands stretch alongside the cliff virtually as far as the eye can see. It's like a small piece of paradise with views over to the small sister island of La Graciosa. At the end of the beach lies the small village of La Caleta de Famara and this marks the end of this trail.

POINTS OF INTEREST

Bosquecillo

This small area at the top of the Famara cliffs offers the perfect place to enjoy spectacular views across to the Chinijo Archipelago and Famara beach. It was reforested with red-eyed wattle trees (*Acacia cyclops*) and Canary wild olive trees (*Olea cerasformis*) and we can also enjoy the beauty of different species of native flowers and plants such as the Famara daisy (Argyranthemun maderense) the fennel-like tajasnoyos (*Ferula lancerottensis*) and the yellow flowered endemic tojio (*Asteriscus intermedius*).

The Famara spring and water galleries

The ancient inhabitants of the island had knowledge of the natural spring at Famara so it was no fortuitous coincidence that lead to the building of the Las Mercedes hermitage here in 1413. In the seventeenth century a small well-like structure was added to the spring to serve as a watering hole for goats and from that moment on, it became known as the La Poceta spring. It became a place of pilgrimage visited by many inhabitants to collect water in times of drought. The water galleries were drilled out at the beginning of the twentieth century and managed to collect an impressive 5 litres of water per minute. In the mid twentieth century more galleries were sunk, these were designed to channel the water flow into two branches collecting nearly 362,000 litres of water per day. (754 of the now obsolete Canarian measurement *pipas*). The water from this gallery and the others in the cliff side were channelled down to Arrecife through pipe work that was built in 1953.

Walk 8 — Costa Teguise - Arrieta

Difficulty rating: moderate
Type: linear
Approximate distance:
18 kilometres
Approximate timing:
4 hours 30 minutes
Terrain gradient:
131 131
Signposting: only some small 'PR' trails marked yellow and white.

Departure point:
Costa Teguise
UTM:
28 R6481173209316
Finishing point:
Arrieta
UTM:
28 R6494483223705

The Ancones coastline offers a variety of landscapes. To one side is the Atlantic Ocean with its constant motion; at times rough, at others calm, and on the other side you have desert-like plains which lie motionless, just waiting for a drop of rain to fall and enable the circle of life to continue in the plants and animals that inhabit the region.

It is a vast area dotted with small coastal villages like Los Ancones, Los Cocoteros and Charco del Palo. The panoramic views throughout the trail allow walkers to see a variety of animals and plants. You will also see the vestiges of industries that were once important sources of income for the island, like the salt works and cochineal.

La Garita beach.

Walk 8

Walk description

Once in Costa Teguise you need to make for the coastline and follow the path all the way up the coast heading north. Keep going along this pleasant walk until you reach the tiny hamlet of Los Ancones.

Los Ancones-Los Cocoteros

From Los Ancones head towards the sea and then inland again along a trail that takes you up in a north-easterly direction. This first stretch of hilly terrain is the perfect way to enjoy Lanzarote's coastal landscape. The coastline is full of rocky cliffs and sea water pools with clear lines of barnacles that mark the meeting of the sea with the land. To your left, you will see dry, scree-covered terrain with mounds scattered

HOW TO GET THERE

By bus: there are regular public transport links between Arrecife and Costa Teguise.
By road: from Arrecife along the LZ-18

POINTS OF INTEREST

- The Los Agujeros saltworks

113

Costa Teguise - Arrieta

> 'The salt pans, those books of pages without rumours'
>
> **Pedro García Cabrera**
> *Vuelta a la isla*

randomly across the plain and small hillocks which could well have been an ancient kind of volcanic oven. The track then hugs the coast and as you walk, it will start to slope downhill until almost at sea level where the Mulión ravine meets the sea. You will see a green-coloured natural water pool here just before you get to the stone beach. Walk past the pool and look for a dirt track that runs parallel to the coastline always in a northeastly direction. Further ahead a few kilometres you will see a few houses to the right, then the trail takes you to the asphalt road that joins the villages of Guatiza and Los Cocoteros, but you need to turn right just before you get to this road. It is worth stopping to see the patterns of the abandoned salt pans built by Tío Joaquín in 1930. Once on the coastal path, keep walking until you reach a beach with an artificial dam and some small summer houses. Just to the north you will see the Los Agujeros salt pans built in 1940 which are still in use today, producing excellent quality salt. The extraction of seawater takes place with the use of wells located in the western part of the salt works just before the salt evaporation ponds. Originally, the clean natural energy source of wind was used to move the seawater, but nowadays it is powered by motors. Stick to the path between the salt pans and the sea and you will see how the sea has eroded the rocks and left a natural work of art in the shape of amazing rock formations on the coastline.

Los Cocoteros-Charco del Palo

As soon as you enter the village of Los Cocoteros you are welcomed by a seawater pool which fills at

Walk 8

ROUTE PROFILE

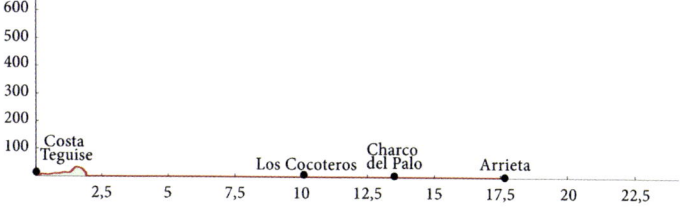

high tide and all but empties at low tide. As you will see, the dam blocking the sea is totally manmade. At the end of the village stands a small monolith with a plaque erected to commemorate those that died in a tragic shipwreck just 20 metres from the coast. Dreams of a new life were extinguished along with the lives of 25 passengers on 17th February 2009 when a small boat carrying men, women and children capsized after crossing the stretch of ocean separating the Lanzarote coast from Africa. The seven survivors were rescued and helped by Los Cocoteros resident, Cristian Hunt.

The dirt track continues parallel to the coast towards a house in front of you. The path to follow is the one that veers off to the left of the house and once this house is behind you, about 30 metres ahead it is worth stopping to look to the right and check out the bubble-like cave (*jameo*) which was formed when the roof of the volcanic tube collapsed, eroded by the force of the sea leaving a natural pool which fills when the strong waves come in. Stick to the coastal path which alternates between being rocky and sandy. The coastline evokes a bygone era when the Moorish pirates would land along this seashore. In fact, even today it is still known as Puerto Moro, or 'Moors' Port'.

LINKS WITH OTHER WALKS

- Arrieta - Haría - Famara (Walk 7)

Charco del Palo - Arrieta

The starting point for this walk is the residential area called Charco del Palo in the municipality of Haría. It is a summer holiday

Costa Teguise - Arrieta

> 'Islands that have coral kisses and pyramids of shadows and volcanic nests for roots...'
>
> **Pedro García Cabrera**
> *Isla sin geografía*

resort for tourists seeking sun, pleasant temperatures and a relaxing day of naturism. You can stop off to pick up supplies at the supermarket or have something to eat or drink in one of the bars. The village is named after the pool of water you can see to the right, where residents and visitors alike can enjoy a refreshing dip to cool off in the summer sun. With the last of the houses behind you, take the white sandy path which runs along the coastline. Keep walking a good while, sticking to the path and ignoring the various smaller paths and trails that run inland and in other directions. The terrain becomes rocky with clay soil from this point. Continue past the Mala pool which can be easily recognised from its artificial cement and stone wall which traps the water at low tide. You can see Mala to the left; together with Guatiza, these two villages were once at the forefront of cochineal production on the island. This was an extremely important industry in the 19th century and was achieved by planting large numbers of prickly pear cactus plants (*Opuntia ficus-indica*) which would be infected with the cochineal beetle in order to produce cochineal which was collected, dried and turned into a natural dye. This colouring was used in all types of industry including the cosmetics, textile and food industries. Today, the cultivation of cochineal has virtually died out as you can see by the fields of cactus that have been left unattended.

Keep walking along the trail parallel to the coast until you reach the bottom end of a property with an abandoned pool and some lime kilns lying in ruins. At one time, lime was an important industry on the island. Master burners would be responsible for burning the limestone to produce lime. It was essential for use in construction as mortar and to paint houses with whitewash made with lime, but it was also used to disinfect the water deposits or to scatter on the vines after pruning to protect from disease. Sticking to the lime kilns, keep to the path which goes up over a small cliff.

Walk 8

Continue parallel to the coast towards an old machine gun nest, but taking the left turn just beforehand. When you are there you will see the La Garita beach open up before your eyes; it is one of the most beautiful beaches on the island. Go down to the beach from the southern end and enjoy a splash in the water before walking on into the town itself; this marks the end of the walk.

POINTS OF INTEREST

Salinas de Los Agujeros

This is one of only two working salt works that are still up and running on the island. It was built in 1940 and covers an area of 45,000 square metres. It is currently undergoing extensive restoration and renovation work. The excellent quality of the salt produced places Lanzarote salt firmly in national and overseas markets.

Walk 9 — Playa Blanca - Janubio

Difficulty rating: easy
Type: linear
Approximate distance: 13 kilometres
Approximate timing: 4 hours
Terrain gradient: 107 ▲ 107 ▲
Signposting: no signposting.
Departure point: Pechiguera lighthouse, Playa Blanca
UTM: 28 R6099823192503
Finishing point: Janubio beach
UTM: 28 R6139173201650

This walk comprises the dry static plains of the south and contrasts them with the coastline in constant motion. The waves pounding away at the rocks, the erosion, salinity, tidal rock pools, small cliffs, blowholes and the spectacular salt pans of Janubio are just some of the impressive sights to behold on this walk which is dominated by the ocean.

The influence of the Atlantic permeates every step of this walk, not just because of its presence and the way it has moulded the landscape, but also in the structures that bear witness to how man has interacted with the ocean; the Pechiguera lighthouse, the old Atlante del Sol hotel and one of Europe's biggest salt works which date back to the late 19th century.

Walk description

This walk starts at the Pechiguera lighthouse in Playa Blanca. The first view you get is of the small islet of Los Lobos and the neighbouring island of Fuerteventura which lies just 14 kilometres away across a stretch of ocean known as La Bocaina. This lighthouse, together with the Martiño lighthouse on Isla de Lobos island and the Tostón on Fuerteventura, helps the boats pass safely through these waters at night. From Pechiguera, take the coastal track northwest. It's a dirt path but you'll have to navigate numerous rocks until you reach a paved avenue.

The coast is battered quite fiercely by the sea here and the waves reach the pools every couple of minutes. When the paved stretch finishes, take the path that runs near the coast. There is a bit of vegetation here, but not much, with just a few

HOW TO GET THERE

By bus: there are regular public transport links between Arrecife and Playa Blanca.
By road: from Arrecife along the LZ-2 and beachfront avenue until the Faro de Pechiguera lighthouse

119

Playa Blanca - Janubio

POINTS OF INTEREST

- The Faro de Pechiguera lighthouse
- The Janubio salt pans

balsamiferous spurge, (*Euphorbia balsamifera*), or *tabaiba* bushes, spiny tea tree shrub (*Licium intricatum*) and Mediterranean saltwort which are relatively bare due to the scarce rainfall and strong salinity in the air because of the sea spray. Some gulls (*Larus michaelis*) will probably keep you company along this stretch.

The Montaña Roja volcanic cone is the only volcano that you will see along this walk. It belongs to the intermediate geological series (II) and was the volcano responsible for creating most of the surface of the southwest of the island with its lava flow.

During the walk you will be able to see lots of seawater pools created as the tide shifts. They may vary in size, but they are all splendid strongholds of biodiversity, where the species

POINT OF INTEREST

Faro de Pechiguera lighthouse
The Pechiguera lighthouse is located in the southwest of the Lanzarote and dates back to 1866 when it was opened as part of the Canary Island Lighting Plan in 1856. It was designed by Juan de León y Castillo who was also the architect behind the Martiño lighthouse on Isla de Lobos and the Punta Delgada lighthouse on the island of Alegranza. It was declared a Cultural Heritage Property in 2002. In 1986 it was replaced by the new Pechiguera lighthouse.

Walk 9

ROUTE PROFILE

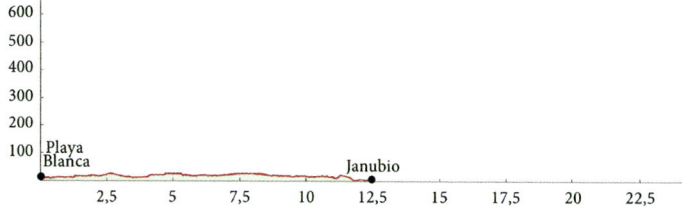

that inhabit them have adapted to the changes in salinity and temperature during their brief few minutes, or sometimes hours, of exposure to the sun and isolation from the sea. There are rock pools which are inhabited by species conditioned by two factors; size and proximity to the sea. Some fish which are often to be seen inlcude the rock goby (*Gobius paganellus*) and the rock-pool blenny (*Parablennius parvicornis*). However, in the bigger pools it is possible to see other species, some of which are edible, and some invertebrates like sea urchins, starfish, brittle stars, caridean shrimp and crab which can be readily found, especially in rock pools covered with seaweed.

This coastal area is named "Los Charcones" after the spectacular rock pools that are formed naturally in the region. A note of warning when exploring these rock pools, though; it is best not to forget this is the Atlantic Ocean and it crashes on the shore with considerable force here; a force that can often catch you unawares if you are not careful.

As you keep walking you will pass the abandoned *Atlante* del Sol hotel; the result of a failed attempt to create a tourist resort here at the beginning of the 1970s. Its failure to take off has left behind a skeleton, an almost ghost-like building which is a blot on this otherwise spectacular landscape. The path hugs the coastline, but it is rocky underfoot, so go carefully to avpid tripping up. At this point you will arrive at the central part of this sweeping bay known as the Rincón del Palo. If you stop and listen, you will hear the roar of a nearby blowhole - it is an

LINKS WITH OTHER WALKS

- Timanfaya Coastline (Walk 10)

The abandoned Atlante del Sol hotel.

121

Playa Blanca - Janubio

Janubio beach.

> 'I have been a labourer all my life
> but there are days when I can't even afford a square meal;
>
> Whilst others dress in their finery and ride good horses;
> theirs are hands that have never seen calluses.'
>
> **Víctor Fernández**
> 'Verses by Víctor Fernández' (salt worker and poet)

impressive sound and sight as the force of the waves pushes the sea up through a crack in the craggy coastline. The dirt track then takes you along the coast called Las Maretas, named after a farmstead of the same name on your right.

The sound of a building emitting machine noises close by is a reminder that we are on an island with no natural water source, so our water has to be extracted from the sea using a desalination process; the machinery you hear belongs to the desalination plant for the south of the island which is housed here. The seawater is converted into drinking water by a system of reverse osmosis and is then pumped into the public supply network.

The trail continues between the sea and the desalination plant and keeps heading north towards Janubio beach. When arriving at the beach you are greeted by a huge expanse of black volcanic sand with waves beating fiercely on the shore, reminding us that this space once formed part of the ocean but was claimed by the lava spill from Timanfaya which created the natural lagoon to your right. This lagoon was once a natural port that disappeared when the entire

Walk 9

coastline was transformed after the volcanic eruptions in Timanfaya. The salt works were built towards the end of the 19th century. It was one of as many as twenty salt works which were dedicated to salt production. The salt industry was a vital part of Lanzarote's economy at one time. The salt was mainly used to preserve pork meat and fish caught in the Canarian-Saharan fishing stocks. Expansion of the salt works came to an end in the middle of the 20th century leaving an enormous area of salt pans measuring some 400,000 square metres.

At the end of the beach there is a car park and this marks the end of the walk.

Alternative route: Janubio salt works

From the northernmost point of Janubio beach you can head east, towards the inner edge of the salt works which lie before you like a beautiful checkerboard garden. The

Janubio salt works.

Playa Blanca - Janubio

unparalleled beauty of the landscape has been crafted by man and encompasses a multitude of ethnographic, cultural, heritage and environmental values. The salt works are still in use today, but production stands at a fraction of what was once generated in their heyday (a mere 10%). Follow the path and pass a house that is virtually in ruins; this is where they placed the motors that pumped the water from the main collection point to feed the salt evaporation ponds.

As you walk, you can see the difference between the salt evaporation ponds and the salt pans. The salt evaporation ponds, or *cocederos* are the large rectangles where the seawater is initially collected for it to evaporate and salinize

The Janubio salt works

These are private salt works that have been producing salt since 1895 and they are still in production today. They are owned by the descendents of Jaime Lleó and the Cerdeña family. Their 440,000 m2 make them the largest salt works in the Canary Islands and they produce 13,000 tonnes of salt per year which is equal to the entire production of all the other salt works on the island combined. Janubio is still in use today, but production is a fraction of what it once was at a mere 10% of what used to be generated. Salt from Janubio is a quality product that is held in high regard in the culinary world.

Photograph from the 1950s with kind permission of Javier Reyes Acuña.

quickly. The concentrated salt water from these pans is channelled to the salt pans (*tajos*) which are the smaller squares which give the checkerboard effect, where the crystallisation takes place. When the salt is extracted it is heaped into large piles before being transported to the salt storage area to the east of the salt works before being packaged and sold. The ruins of old windmills at the site are vestiges of an age when the water would have been pumped from the lagoon into the evaporation ponds by wind power. Janubio is an ideal spot for lovers of birding as you can capture stunning images of birdlife such as Kentish plovers, grey plovers, ruddy turnstones, herons, whimbrels, common greenshanks, black-winged stilt, and ruddy shelduck.

The return walk follows the same route; in this direction the pink colour of the salt evaporation ponds stands out, this is due to algae like the *Dunaliela salina* which are capable of living in highly saline atmospheres and the archaea microorganisms *Halobacterium salinarum* and *H. halobium*. You can also stop and try to spot the brine shrimp (*Artemia salina*), a miniscule crustacean (8-13mm) which looks a bit like a prawn that thrives in these saline conditions.

These are the largest and most visually stunning salt works in the Canary Islands. They are protected under Decree-Law 1/2000 as a Place of Scientific Interest.

> 'The lake at Janubio is the embodiment of Lanzarote's marine soul.
> A chunk of blue stolen from the ocean.'
>
> **Agustín Espinosa**
> *Lancelot 28º-7º*

Walk 10 — Timanfaya Coastline

Difficulty rating: challenging
Type: linear
Approximate distance: 12 kilometres
Approximate timing: 4 hours 30 minutes
Terrain gradient: 108 ⛰ 117 ⛰
Signposting: no signposting.
Departure point: Playa de la Madera beach (Tinajo coast)
UTM: 28 R6193323215482
Finishing point: El Golfo
UTM: 28 R6138363206890

The walk along the Timanfaya coastline resembles terrain you associate more with a distant planet than with planet earth. On the one side of you is a vast sea of dark, motionless lava whilst opposite is the vast Atlantic Ocean; at times raging and at others calm, but either way in constant motion as if in a bid to recoup the terrain it lost to the volcanoes during the eruptions in the 18th century.

It is a volcanic trail set to the soundtrack of silent lava fields and the tumultuous sea. You will be walking through the Timanfaya National Park so despite there being no really steep climbs or ascents, hikers should take care and be prepared to tackle the jagged terrain.

Walk 10

Walk description

The best way to reach the beginning of this trail is in your own vehicle, driving from Tinajo along *calle la Laguneta*. Drive out of the village in a westerly direction along an asphalt road towards the village of Tenésar for approximately 4 kilometres. It is a tiny coastal settlement belonging to the municipality of Tinajo where locals traditionally spend their summer holidays. You will reach a crossroads with the asphalt road turning to the right and a dirt road straight ahead - take this track, always heading west and ignoring all other forks for 6 kilometres until you reach the La Madera beach. Park up here, taking care not to leave any valuables on show inside your vehicle.

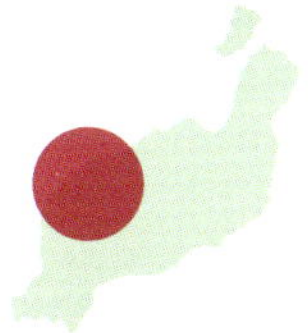

HOW TO GET THERE

By bus: there is just one regular bus service between Arrecife and Tinajo.

By road: from Arrecife along the LZ-20 and *calle Laguneta* road.

POINT OF INTEREST

- Timanfaya National Park

127

Playa de La Madera - Playa del Cochino

Playa de La Madera is a black sandy beach with strong currents that make it rather dangerous, like most beaches on the northwest coast of Lanzarote. Sadly the beach is littered with plastic, wood and old nets; this is rubbish swept up onto the beach after being dumped by humans on another coast or even out at sea. These flotsam and jetsam are known on the island as j*allos*.

The walk now crosses the beach and at the western end you will see a path that runs parallel to the coast and which you need to stick to all the way to the end of the trail. The rough volcanic terrain underfoot is the legacy of the series of eruptions in Timanfaya in the 18th century. They formed a totally new surface covering nearly a third of the whole island and increasing the surface area of this coastal region on which you are now walking. This parallel path is totally flat but what makes it tricky for walkers is the instability of the terrain with loose rocks and scree underfoot. Before setting off, you should ensure you are wearing strong, hard-wearing walking boots and that you have sun protection cream and plenty of water with you as this is an isolated area with no services or road links nearby.

Virtually your only company along this volcanic and maritime walk is the sound of the sea battering

ROUTE PROFILE

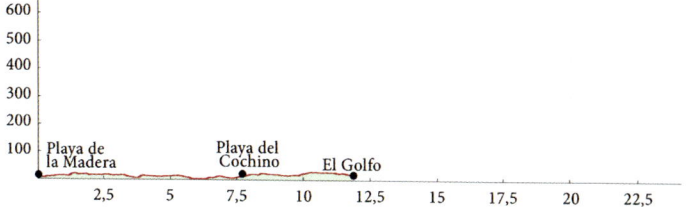

the coast. If the sea is rough you will be rewarded with the spectacular vision of huge crests of water and white foam splashing against the black volcanic rock. To the right you have the blues and turquoises of the sea and to the left the black tones of the lava fields. Before long, you will reach the outskirts of Timanfaya National Park, at points it might seem that the footpath disappears, but just look up and ahead and you will see how the path continues just a few metres further on; you can be reassured that the path never veers away from the coast, it always runs close to the coastline. The Playa del Cochino beach marks roughly the halfway point of the walk (8 kilometres). Its black sand provides welcome relief to weary feet after walking over lava fields. There are many rock pools in the area and they are occasionally visited by fishermen and shellfish gatherers from neighbouring villages and they sometimes build makeshift shacks out of the flotsam and jetsam that wash up onto the shore. The Playa del Cochino beach is a perfect place to rest, gather your strength and cool off by dipping your toes into one of the many rock pools.

Playa del Cochino beach - El Golfo

The vast rivers of lava that were once molten and now petrified are testament to the dramatic series of eruptions that took place on the island some 300 years ago. The wrath of the volcanoes left behind dark, barren wastelands of solidified

LINKS WITH OTHER WALKS

- Caldera Blanca (Walk 15)

- Playa Blanca - Janubio (Walk 10)

Timanfaya Coastline

Flotsam and jetsam on the Playa el Cochino beach.

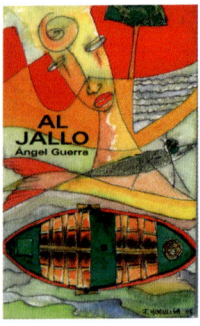

Cover of the book entitled "Al Jallo" designed by Félix Hormiga (see page 148).

lava that are too harsh to sustain much life. It is bereft of nutrients, with no traces of fertile soil left and the influence of the sea spray makes it virtually impossible for any life forms to survive. Keep heading south, the path that takes you along the coast will soon appear before you. Stop for a minute and watch how the dramatic sea spray dances in the air as it thrashes the rocks in this constant battle between land and sea.

In the distance on the left you will start to make out the Islote de Halcones - a rise that was part of the mountain that stood long before the eruptions in Timanfaya and which remained intact even after the eruptions, so providing a natural safe haven for all its flora and fauna. Keep walking and at the top of the rise the path starts to go slightly inland until it gets to a dirt track and an intersection of paths; the one to the left takes you out of Timanfaya National Park alongside Montaña Quemada and the one to the right takes you to the El Paso beach. Ignore both of these options, however, and go straight ahead to walk inland towards another volcanic rise called el Mojón.

You are in an area dominated by spurge, Mediterranean saltwort, barbed wire bushes, southern tea trees and endemic verode succulents. The path zigzags up with a few twists and turns and after a gentle ascent you will find yourself on the edge of the cliff on top of El Paso beach. This is a really important ornithological spot as it is the nesting site for the Cory's shearwater, amongst other seabirds. Beneath you are sizeable volcanic tubes, in fact, in one of them (the Chifletera Cave), human remains belonging to the indigenous population have been found.

When leaving Timanfaya National Park you will see the coastal village and mountain of El Golfo to the south. You will enter from the northern end by a children's play park. To be able to see the mountain and the Charco de los Clicos lagoon, you will need to walk right through the village heading south. It is well worth stopping in one of the restaurants here to try the fresh fish and traditional wrinkly potatoes. This is the end of the walk.

Walk 10

POINTS OF INTEREST

Timanfaya National Park

This area was declared a National Park on 9th August 1974 by Decree 2615/1974 and reclassified by the 6/1981 Law of 25th March. It is a vast area measuring 51km2 which includes volcanic cones, lava flows, fields of volcanic ash which date back to the 18th century and 19th century eruptions. There are also two rises (Kipuka) like the Islote de Halcones and the Islote El Mojón which are home to animals and vegetation that pre-date the eruptions. The Park extends over areas in the municipal regions of Yaiza and Tinajo. 96% of the land is owned by these municipalities and the remaining 4% is in private hands. More than 90% of the park has been declared a Reserve Zone and as such enjoys the maximum possible protection ensuring that it can only be used for scientific and environmental purposes. The area allocated for Special Use is the part dedicated to tourism which attracts (1,500,000 people per year) with places like the Taro, Islote del Hilario, the camel walk and camel station, and the Volcano route. Visitors are first greeted at the top of the Islote del Hilario rise where they are treated to the spectacular site of geysers as they spew water rapidly heated by the geothermic heat underfoot and the burning of the barbed-wire bushes (*Launaea arborescens*) which rapidly set fire due to the heat of the earth just a few centimetres below the surface. In the restaurant they actually cook some food in an oven and over a barbecue grill using this natural heat. The El Diablo restaurant and the guided bus tour through the park, the so-called 'Volcano Route', are fruit of a joint design collaboration between Jesús Soto and César Manrique. The National Park also offers three of its own guided walks; the Tremesana walk, the El Golfo walk and the Timanfaya Coastline walk.

Walk 11 — The Volcán de La Corona Volcano

Difficulty rating: easy
Type: circular
Approximate distance: 3 kilometres
Approximate timing: 1 hour 30 minutes
Terrain gradient: 134 134
Signposting: no signposting.
Departure/Finishing point: Ye, San Francisco Church
UTM: 28 R6474143230607

Suitable for families with children

This is a relatively young volcanic cone located in the municipality of Haría and its summit rewards hikers with some amazing views across the northern part of the island. It is an impressive sight from sea level too as its presence dominates Lanzarote's north. The shape of the Volcán de La Corona, its crater, colouring and extensive lava fields have together been declared a Protected Natural Area and are a designated Natural Monument.

The volcanic tube which created the Cueva de los Verdes cave system and the Jameos del Agua emerges beneath the flank of the mountain and runs all the way to the coast.

This is a perfect walk for the whole family as it is short and easily accessible.

Walk 11

Walk description

The walk starts at the San Francisco Javier church in the village of Ye. The aim is to reach the La Corona volcanic cone (604 m) that can be seen to the south. It is a volcano that erupted some 18,000 years ago, approximately, and created the vast lava field that is known as *malpaís*, or 'badlands'. This sea of solidified lava considerably increased the surface area of the island in the northeast and it can be seen from Órzola to Arrieta. This walk takes you east along the LZ-20, after 150 metres you need to turn right heading south along a rough volcanic pebble path. Follow this track amongst planted vines in volcanic areas where the ground is rocky with little soil. The farmers toil hard to make the most of the land despite the harsh conditions. You can see walls of volcanic rocks, built to shelter the

HOW TO GET THERE

By bus: there are regular public transport links between Arrecife and Arrieta.
By road: from Arrecife along the LZ-1 and LZ-201 roads.

POINTS OF INTEREST

- The La Corona Natural Monument (continued overleaf)

The Volcán de La Corona Volcano

- The Mirador del Río vantage point
- The Batería del Río gun battery

vines, fig trees and some almond trees. As the trail ascends, it turns into a narrower footpath which takes you to the La Corona crater towards the south. You will pass a solitary palm tree (*Phoenix canariensis*) as you follow the footpath as it snakes up amongst plentiful Canary sorrel shrubs (*Rumex lunaria*) and spurge (*Euphorbia regis jubae*).

When you reach the edge of the crater you will be rewarded with the sight of a spectacular natural amphitheatre with its myriad of reds, blacks, greens and greys that provide a real visual treat. The towering, irregular shape of the edges

POINTS OF INTEREST

Mount Corona Natural Monument

Towering at some 604 m, the La Corona volcano is one of Lanzarote's highest points above sea level and is one of the island's youngest cones. It erupted approximately 18,000 years ago and generated an expansive lava field that swept right across to the northwest coast. The eruption also created the incredible volcanic tube that begins under the cone and runs for 6 kilometres down into the ocean. Some parts of the tube have since collapsed creating open bubbles called *jameos*. The Cueva de los Verdes (the Greens' Cave) and the Jameos del Agua tourist attractions are located in different parts of this tube. They were created in the sixties by visionaries César Manrique and Jesús Soto as stunning places for tourists to visit. The La Corona Natural Monument is protected by Decree-Law 1/2000 and covers an expanse of 1,797.2 hectares.

Walk 11

ROUTE PROFILE

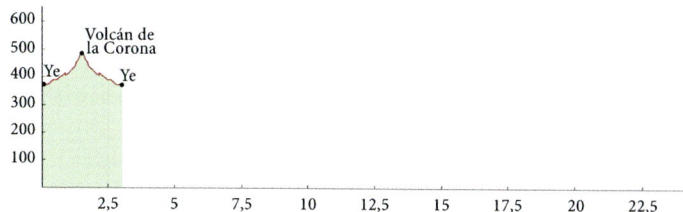

of the crater is reminiscent of of a royal crown. From this same viewpoint you can see part of the Chinijo archipelago if you look northwards with the islands of La Graciosa and Montaña Clara. Standing alone to their east you can see the solitary Roque del Este rock. You will also be able to see some of the vineyard area known as Ye-Lajares and the unusual-looking house of Domingo López Fontes, nicknamed locally as the 'little tower'. In order to get back, you simply need to retrace your steps back to the departure point.

Alternative route
Ye - Mirador and Gun Battery

An alternative walk is to head northwards out of the village from the San Francisco Javier church in Ye along an asphalt road which takes you out of town between farmlands covered in volcanic pebbles (*lapilli*). Being so high up provides the crops with better conditions as it is cooler and more humid. This road comes out at a crossroads with the LZ-202 road which links Ye with the Mirador del Río. You need to cross it, heading east past an old *aljibe* water deposit and then take a dirt track northeast. This track will take you to the edge of the Famara cliff next to the Mirador del Río vantage point. This spectacular lookout point affords visitors stunning views of the whole of the Chinijo Archipelago. You will find yourself standing in what is left of the old military battery of 'el Río', the name given to this stretch of water that separates La Graciosa from Lanzarote. It is recognisable from its series of circular platforms,

LINKS WITH OTHER WALKS

- Órzola - Haría (Walk 1)

- The Graciosa People's Walk (Walk 12)

The Volcán de La Corona Volcano

some steps going underground and a lookout post near the Mirador del Río. This gun battery was installed in 1878 as Spain went to war with the United States. Its purpose was to defend the strait as it might have provided the perfect hideout for enemy naval vessels to weigh anchor in secret. The gun emplacement was never actually put to use and was dismantled after the Second World War.

César Manrique, Jesús Soto and Eduardo Cáceres were the brains behind taking this military installation and remodelling it to create the spectacular vantage point that now stands in its place. Built in 1970, it became a new tourist centre belonging to the Island Council (*Cabildo*). If you carry on walking northeast, you will see more platforms which were once used as bases for the guns to launch shells and mortars. The walk to the northernmost point of the island culminates in breathtaking views with cliffs on either side of you. In order to return to your original departure point, just retrace your footsteps back.

Mirador del Río

This unique lookout point, skilfully integrated into the Famara cliff face, was built in 1969 and officially opened to the public in 1971. It was created by César Manrique in such a way that it is barely perceptible from La Graciosa on the other side of the strait, with ingenious use of design and materials that make it virtually invisible. The architect Eduardo de Cáceres and artist Jesús Soto also collaborated to make Manrique's vision a reality. The Mirador del Río is one of the island's Centres of Art, Culture and Tourism and can be visited from 10am to 5.45 pm in winter and until 6.45 pm from July to September.

Batería del Río Gun Battery

The Río gun battery was built between May and June in 1898 to protect against possible use as an anchorage point by enemy vessels in the Río, the narrow stretch of water between La Graciosa and Lanzarote. In April 1898, the United States declared war against Spain after the explosion of the USS warship, the Maine in Havana. This war would cause Spain to lose Cuba, Puerto Rico, the Philippines and Guam. The fear that the Canary Islands would also be invaded prompted the fortification of this area of Lanzarote and at one time the battery housed four 21 centimetre howitzer guns and two 27 centimetre mortars. This gun battery is situated some 400 metres high in the Famara cliff side and at one time comprised lookout posts, walkways, trenches, dugouts and stores, but it was all dismantled in 1945.

Walk 12 — The People of La Graciosa's Trail

Difficulty rating: challenging
Type: circular (return via the same route)
Approximate distance: 7 kilometres (3.5 kilometres to the El Río salt pans
Approximate timing: 3 hours
Terrain gradient: 380 ▲ 380 ▲
Signposting: no signposting.
Departure/Finishing point: Ye, (calle de Las Rositas Road LZ-202)
UTM: 28 R6465683230688

The walk up and down the cliffs of Famara is also known as the 'The People of La Graciosa's Trail'. It is a steep vertical trail that ascends and descends the Famara cliff face which stands at nearly 500 metres tall. As you descend the cliff you will be able to enjoy the stunning panoramic views across to the island of La Graciosa and the smaller islets that lie at the north of the island, as well as the magnificent beaches and salt pans at the foot of the cliff. This is an area of enormous biodiversity where you will have the chance to see a huge variety of flora and fauna. This footpath was once of great importance as it was used up until relatively recently by those that lived on La Graciosa as their only means of trading goods in Lanzarote. This was a job mainly left to the women and it formed part of their regular routine. They would have to trek up the cliff, laden with their wares such as dried or salted fish to sell or exchange for produce grown in the fields in Lanzarote.

Walk description

The starting point for this walk is the paved car park in *calle Las Rositas* street (the LZ-202 road in Ye) at the top edge of the Famara cliff, close to Finca La Corona rural hotel. The paved footpath takes you west with some steps that lead to a vantage point that affords super views of the cliffs, the lower foothills and the salt pans as well as the Chinijo Archipelago. The downward hike takes you zigzagging all the way, gradually covering some 400 metres of cliff face. You will see the different layers of stratification in the cliff which reveal that it originates from a shield type volcano. The possible explanation behind the formation of these cliffs is that they may have been the result of a geological shift which forced part of this volcano into the sea. The path takes you over a sea of lava from Montaña La Corona

HOW TO GET THERE

By bus: there are regular public transport links between Arrecife and Ye.
By road: from Arrecife along the LZ-1, LZ-201 and LZ-202 roads.

POINTS OF INTEREST

- The Chinijo Archipelago National Park

139

The People of La Graciosa's Trail

Orchella Weed
(*Roccella canariensis*):
Is a lichen which produces dye that was used by the ancient Romans, Genoese and Venetian textile producers in the 15th century. It is possible that the presence of plentiful supplies of orchella weed may well have been the reason behind the conquest of the Canary Islands by Jean de Bethencourt.

which flowed over this cliff and generated a younger surface layer which is lower down and darker in tone. The flora and fauna found in this landscape cannot be seen anywhere else on the planet as it is home to the vast majority of the island's endemic species. You can see a native species of lavender (*Lavandula pinnata*), spurge (*Euphorbia regis-jubae*) and you might be lucky and see a Barbary falcon (*Falco pelegrinoides*) swoop across your path or maybe even an Egyptian vulture (*Neophron percnopterus*). If you have a good look at the rocks, you will see that they are covered with lichen; this plant-like organism is part fungus and part algae and capable of living on rocks, with no fertile soil. The orchella weed is one such species of lichen which was particularly important in the past as it could supply a purple coloured dye.

Back on the walk; when you get to the bottom, the path takes you northeast towards the idyllic *Bajorrisco* beach set in stunning, isolated surroundings and where a narrow stretch of water, just over 1 kilometre wide separates you from the island of La Graciosa.

Once you have recovered your strength after a well-earned rest and a splash in the sea, you can head northeast to the El Río salt pans - they are

POINTS OF INTEREST

The Chinijo Archipelago National Park

It became a designated Protected Natural Area in 1986 and was reclassified by the 12/1994 Law in 1994 (now contained in Decree-Law 1/2000) and encompasses two different areas.

On the one side stands the Protected Natural Park which includes the smaller islets to the north of Lanzarote; Alegranza, La Graciosa, Montaña Clara, Roque del Este and Roque del Oeste; and on the other side it covers the cliffs of Famara, the strip of sandy land between the cliffs and Soo and the mountains of Soo. It is an area that is home to the greatest range of biodiversity on Lanzarote and contains virtually all the island's endemic botanical species. In addition, it is the nesting area of important birdlife such as the Egyptian vulture (*Neophron peropterus*), the Ealonora's falcon (*Falco eleonorae*), the Barbary falcon (*Falco pelegrinoides*) and the Cory's Shearwater (*Calonectris diomedea*).

Walk 12

ROUTE PROFILE

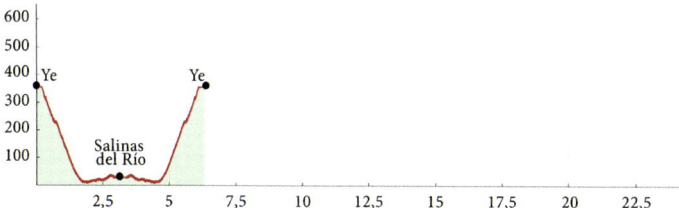

the oldest in the Canaries, dating back to the 16th century. They are an amazing colour and were used up until recently to obtain salt for the fish processing industry. This is a popular haunt for different species of waders. If you look east, you will see a patch of green vegetation in the distance; this marks the spot of the natural Gusa spring which has provided a much sought after source of fresh water since ancient times. The return leg of the walk will take you exactly the same way back; make sure you have recouped your strength ready to take the tricky ascent cautiously and at your own pace. Whilst this is a leisure activity for you today, it is humbling to remember that the tough climb up and down this path was once a compulsory part of survival for the inhabitants of La Graciosa. They would have to haul kilos of dried salted fish up the cliff to take to market and trade for produce from the farms on Lanzarote and they would have to descend once more, laden with their food to return to their little island. This hard task was mainly carried out by the women of the island and we at this guide book would like to pay tribute to all those brave and hardy women.

LINKS TO OTHER WALKS

- La Corona (Walk 11)

- Órzola - Haría (Walk 1)

Walk 13 — Historical Teguise

Difficulty rating: easy
Type: circular
Approximate distance: 1.2 kilometres
Approximate timing: 1 hour
Terrain gradient: 10 ▲ 10 ▲
Signposting: most of the historical buildings have explanatory plaques.
Departure/Finishing point: Plaza de La Constitución square (Teguise)
UTM: 28 R6401703215413

Suitable for families and users of joëlettes or specially adapted wheelchairs.

A walk through the historical centre of Teguise transports you several centuries back in time to an era when it was the capital of Lanzarote, the island was ruled by feudal lords of the *Ancien Regime* and ecclesiastical power reigned supreme. The architectural features add to its historical air with buildings that mostly date back to the 18th and 19th centuries. In 1852 its status as island capital was rescinded in favour of Arrecife. This put a stop to its heyday of growth and power that it had enjoyed in previous centuries and meant an economic crisis that put a halt to any new constructions. This rather ironically meant that Teguise has been preserved as one of the most picturesque historical towns in the Canarian archipelago and one of great cultural value. Exploring its streets, admiring its houses, monasteries and churches and learning about some of its famous personalities helps us relive the history of Lanzarote. This is a lovely walk in a quiet town, steeped in history and local culture.

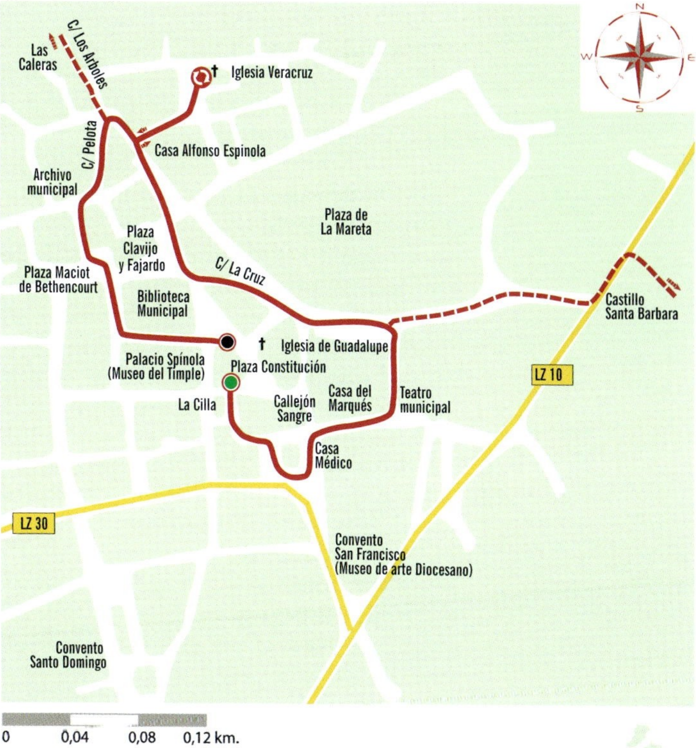

Walk description

Starting from the central *Plaza de La Constitución* square, this walk takes you through the historical centre of Teguise, declared Historic-Artistic site in 1985 thanks to its rich architecture and to it being one of the best preserved old towns left in the Canaries. It became the capital of the island after the conquest and the feudal lords moved in. It was the third city to be founded by the Europeans in the Canary Islands after Rubicón and Betancuria. It was Maciot de Bethencourt who chose this exceptional central location; far away from the coast and possible pirate attacks. The religious orders followed in his footsteps building churches and monasteries. The Nuestra Señora de Guadalupe Church stands in the *Plaza de La Constitución* square. It was built in 1455 as the Mother Church and therefore it soon became the

HOW TO GET THERE

-By bus: regular public transport connections between Arrecife and Teguise
-By car: the LZ-1 and LZ-10 take you there

OF INTEREST

The vast majority of buildings mentioned are places of interest.
- Teguise
- Legend of Ico
(continued overleaf)

Historical Teguise

- Alfonso Spínola and Ángel Guerra
- The Diabletes
- Virgin of Guadalupe
- Pelotamano handball

WHAT TO VISIT

- The Convento Santo Domingo Monastery
This monastery was built at the beginning of the 18th century on the foundations of the church that had stood there a century before. The residential area for the friars was next door; where the town hall is located today. The old San Juan de Diós and San Francisco de Padua church has since been converted and now houses an exhibition hall for occasional special events.

-Casa Museo Marqués de Herrera y Rojas House/Museum
This house was built in 1929 by Luis Ramírez González on the foundations of an old 18th century house. During this rebuild, the heartwood door and the stone work of the doorway were relocated from the original Herrera y Rojas palace and placed on the front of this new building.

religious hub of the city. However, throughout its long history it has suffered numerous pirate attacks when it has been plundered and razed to the ground on several occasions. The last fire was in 1909 and after its last restoration it was turned into a neo-gothic, somewhat cold building that bears no resemblance to any of the other churches on the island. Its bell tower was also raised making Teguise clearly visible from far away.

The *Plaza de La Constitución* square has been a central part of Teguise life for time immemorial, although it was previously called the San Miguel square. In the 1940s it underwent remodelling work and the fountain was installed, along with the benches which were made from stones brought from the Arucas quarry in Gran Canaria; this was achieved thanks to the support of the locals and special participation of Luis Ramírez González who invested in the refurbishment. There is also a bronze sculpture by local artist Rigoberto Camacho in homage to the folk musical tradition of the *Ranchos de Pascua* music groups. It is a tradition inherited from the ancient *Ranchos de Ánimas* who would play in the streets and collect alms. The *Ranchos de Pascua* tradition has been kept alive and these music groups can still be seen during Christmas celebrations today.

On one side of the square is the Spínola Palace; once a family home owned by the Feo Peraza family and headquarters too of the dreaded Inquisition. A descendent of this family married Ángel Spínola in the 20th century so giving it its name. From 1989 it was the official head office of the Canarian Government, but today it is home to the Timple Museum; a museum dedicated to the four-stringed Canarian musical instrument that has deep-rooted traditions in this old city. Teguise holds a special place in the hearts of *timple* players across the Canaries, as it is where many master *timple* makers have their workshops and craft their instruments.

On the other side of the *Plaza* is *La Cilla*, or tithe barn, which was built in 1680 to store grain that was collected from the Church's own lands

Walk 13

ROUTE PROFILE

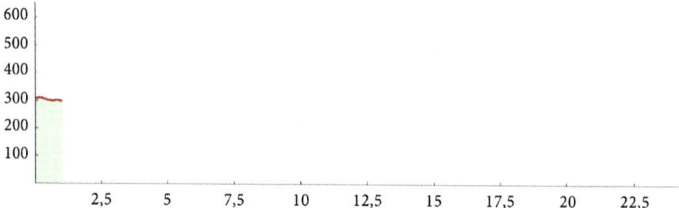

and the collection of the tithe tax (a tenth part of someone's produce or income which they give or pay as tax to the Church.) Today it houses a bank after it was restored in 1986 with the collaboration of César Manrique. Along the left hand side of the tithe barn you can take the *calle Reyes Católicos* street and after about 40 metres you will find the *Casa del Médico* (Doctor's House) where the *Plaza de San Francisco* square once stood. Its construction was promoted by the Canary Island's Economic Council Organisation, together with the Ministry of the Interior, the Falange and the Lanzarote *Cabildo* (Island Council) in 1954. In front of the house there is another bronze sculpture, also created by artist Rigoberto Camacho in honour of the *Diabletes de Teguise*. These 'Little devils of Teguise' have long formed part of local Carnival tradition in which men and young boys dress up in white costumes painted with red and black diamonds. They also wear a facemask with horns and an overlarge tongue - a scary cross between bull and devil - their aim is to 'terrorise' the streets wielding a pole with a sand-filled pouch attached with which to give kids and adults a playful bash. The *diabletes* imitate the sound of a male goat as they bleat loudly and run around ringing their cowbells and rattles. In olden times they would dance and chase through the streets on the night of the 31st December and on Corpus Christi.

Beside you now you will see the long facade of an old house where bars, restaurants and shops now stand. They are actually part of what was at

LINKS WITH OTHER WALKS

- Haría - Teguise (Walk 2)

- Teguise - Tias (Walk 3)

Historical Teguise

The Diabletes of Teguise

At Carnival time the *Diabletes* are familiar figures on the island, and in Teguise in particular. They are the product of a cultural mix of beliefs; with influences from the indigenous islanders, a touch of mainland Spain together with African influences from the Moorish slaves brought to the island in the 5th and 6th centuries.

one time the monks' quarters connected to the San Francisco monastery built in 1588. To the far right you have the old Nuestra Señora de Miraflores church which has now been converted into the San Francisco monastery's Diocesan Museum of Sacred Art.

To continue with the walk, just pop back to *calle Los Reyes Católicos* street and in front of you, you will see a narrow lane called Callejón de la Sangre or 'Blood Alley' - so called because a river of blood flowed down the alley as the locals fought to defend themselves against the marauding attacks of Arráez the pirate. Continue up *calle Herrera y Rojas* street named after the lords and marquis who lived in the stately home to your left. After it was rebuilt in the 19th century the rather basic house was converted into the six houses that stand here today. Inside there are various curiosities worth taking a look at; such as ancient stones engraved with rustic images of footprints (podomorphs) which predate the Spanish conquest of the island. Agustín de Herrera y Rojas was the name of a dynasty of lords (father, son and grandson) who governed this island state during the 17th and 18th centuries. Walk up *calle Espíritu Santo* street named after the church that once stood

POINTS OF INTEREST

Teguise

The city was founded by Maciot de Bethencourt around the mid 15th century and built on the foundations of an indigenous settlement called Acatife. Maciot was the nephew of Jean de Bethencour, the conqueror and first feudal lord of Lanzarote. Teguise was the centre for civil and military government of the island which was overseen as a small state. Different ecclesiastical orders established churches and monasteries in this centre, some of which can still be seen today. It was located in a strategically advantageous position as it was in the centre of the island and far inland from the coast and possible pirate attacks. It also had a *mareta* - a large water reservoir that would collect rain water that ran off the sides of Mount Guanapay. Once the water was collected in the *mareta* it would be shared out as needed. Teguise was first governed by the Bethencourts and then by the Herrera family who promoted the development of Teguise by capturing slaves from the nearby African coast and putting them to work on the island. This generated economic movement that attracted the interest of pirates who attacked and plundered on various occasions. Years later, the advent of the *barrilla* (saltwort) industry (*Mesembrianthemum crystallinum*) created important trade links in the port of Arrecife and in so doing transferred economic power to this port. Arrecife claimed its status as capital and years after the episodes of civil unrest known as the *Guerra Chica* (1810), the change of capital to Arrecife became official.

The Legend of Ico

In 1377, a Spanish Navy vessel captained by Martín Ruiz de Avendaño stopped off in Lanzarote. The Chief-King of the *Majos*, Zonzamas, granted an audience with the Biscayan captain and having established his good intentions, the king offered him shelter and invited him to sleep in his settlement. According to legend, Martín Ruiz de Avendaño received the amorous attentions of Queen Faina during his stay.

The captain took his leave and his ship set sail, leaving behind a pregnant Queen Faina who nine months later gave birth to a little girl with blonde hair and fair skin. Her appearance obviously gave rise to rumours that she was not the fruit of King Zonzamas's loins. Her name was Ico and she was heir to the throne but her fellow island folk doubted the purity of her royal blood line and forced her to undertake the smoke challenge. The test consisted of placing her in a cave together with three girls from the lowest social caste. They lit a fire at the entrance to the cave and wafted the smoke inside. If Princess Ico survived then it would be proven that she was the true daughter of Zonzamas. The legend has it that before entering the cave, Ico's nanny, Uga, who was also the local witchdoctor, gave her a sponge soaked in water to cover her nose and mouth. Ico took her advice and subsequently she emerged from the cave alive and well so she was hailed queen.

Historical Teguise

Ángel Guerra

The politician and journalist José Betancort Cabrera (Teguise 1874 - Madrid 1950) wrote under the pseudonym Ángel Guerra. In his novels he wrote about life on the island at the end of the 19th century and at the turn of the twentieth century. Two of his best-known works are; "La Lapa" and "El Jallo".

there back in 1730. It later became the hospital and children's home and its function changed yet again in 1825 when it became, and still remains, the Teguise municipal theatre.

Once you have come to the end of this street, turn left and you will be in the *La Mareta* plaza where Teguise's *mareta* once stood. A *mareta* being a huge water deposit which collected the water that ran off *Mount Guanapay*. It was in use long ago by the indigenous population, the *majos*, and continued to be used until the 1960s when it fell into disrepair and was demolished. From this point, walk down *calle Cruz* and you will see one of the 14 crosses that can be found in the historical centre of Teguise which represent the 14 Stations of the Cross. This one in particular has an inscription at its base with the name Francisco Delgado - he was the man who donated this cross back in 1909. Today, the tradition of adorning the crosses with flowers has been revived and this is carried out around the Day of the Holy Cross (3rd May).

When you reach the Clavijo y Fajardo plaza, you will see a sculpture which represents water collection - a harsh and demanding part of the island's culture. Beside it is another sculpture, this one by artisan José Aradas which was placed to commemorate Andrés Parrilla and his fellow shipmates who were killed in a terrorist attack when they were fishing in the Canarian-Saharan fishing banks in 1978.

This plaza is surrounded by beautiful buildings;

one of them is the Díaz house which now houses the Teguise municipal library. Another interesting house is that of Mr. Eligio which is currently a shop, but up high on the facade you can see chiselled in stone the word *Hospital*. This stone comes from the old Espiritu Santo hospital which is now the local theatre. Carry on walking up *calle José Antonio* and you will see one side the Palacio Ico building dating from the 18th century. It was once the headquarters of the Civil Guard and it is now named after Princess Ico, a legendary princess of the indigenous population. On the other side stands the birthplace of famous writer José Betancort Cabrera who wrote under the pseudonym Ángel Guerra. You will then get to *calle Alfonso Spínola* where it is worth stopping to admire the large windows which mark the house where the prestigious doctor Alfonso Spínola was born.

In *calle Vera Cruz* you will see the 17th century church of the same name. This church became a venerated centre of worship in Teguise owing to the fact that it housed the statue of the Most Holy Christ on the Cross brought from Portugal. Today you can see this Christ on the Cross with a head of natural long hair in the Guadalupe church in the main square. You can choose whether to walk down *calle Norte* or retrace your steps back up Alfonso Spínola street to *calle Rayo* where you can see the aptly named *calle los Árboles* with its beautiful twisted pepper trees (*Schinus molle*) whose green canopies provide some welcome shade.

You now need to head along *calle Pelota* which takes its name from the old Lanzarote sporting tradition of handball or *pelotamano*. Then turn right along *calle Carnicería* heading west where you will get to the municipal archive. This old stately home dating back to the 18th century is known as the 'Perdomo House' and was converted into the historical archive back in 1990. It stores the majority of documents about the history, geography, economy and religion of Lanzarote and its inhabitants.

From here along *calle Correo*, you reach the *Maciot de Bethencourt* plaza, named after the governor of the island at the beginning of the fifteenth century. Here you can still see the old water fountain installed thanks to the implementation of

Alfonso Spínola

(*Teguise 1845 - San José, Uruguay 1905*) Spínola studied medicine in Cádiz (1869) and returned to Teguise where he worked as a doctor for eight years. He then married Rosalía Spínola and emigrated to Uruguay with their three children. He dedicated his life to medicine and he even managed to cure smallpox epidemics by attending to patients in his house. He was the appointed doctor in charge in many towns including Montevideo, Las Piedras, and San José, and he founded the first microbiological laboratory in Uruguay called the Dr. Ferrán laboratory. He was also professor at different teaching institutes. His children followed his footsteps into research, studying history, natural history and languages. Spínola was passionate about his work in the medical profession and was well known and admired for never discriminating between rich or poor.

Historical Teguise

The Virgin of Guadalupe

The story of the Virgin of Guadalupe statuette is as full of trials and tribulations as the Mother church which takes its name. This image of Our Lady of Guadalupe was brought to Teguise by Diego García de Herrera back in the fifteenth century. It was later plundered and the head decapitated by North African pirates. However, in a twist of fate, the head was rescued by a captive slave from Lanzarote who managed to escape and return with the head. After it was restored, it was given a safe haven in the Las Nieves hermitage. After the fire of the original church in Teguise in 1909, it was decided that she should return to take her place in Teguise's mother church.

the Teguise Water Supply Plan of 1961. From here you can walk along *calle Higuera* street passing a plaque in honour of writer José Betancort Cabrera who once lived there. Turn up *calle Nueva* and you will be back in the *Plaza de La Constitución*. This is the end of the walk.

Alternative routes

Teguise - Santa Bárbara Castle (1,6 kilometres)

Starting from the *Plaza de La Mareta*, walk up towards an old windmill which at one time would have been used to mill toasted grain. Walk up *calle Garajonay* heading east and be careful as you cross the busy *Gran Aldea* main road. Here you are at the barrier which marks the entrance to the drive up to the Santa Bárbara castle, which today houses the Pirate Museum. It is a 1.5 kilometre walk up a relatively steep asphalt road until you reach the ancient castle on top of the old Guanapay volcano. It was a strategically advantageous location for this oldest military fortress on Lanzarote because of its natural vantage point across much of the island. There is some debate as to when exactly it was built, with some scholars saying that Lancelotto Malocello actually built a watchtower here in 1312. What is known for certain is that Sancho de Herrera built a tower here in the 16th century and that it was later in the sixteenth century that the Italian engineer Torriani designed the castle as it now stands. The fortification was designed to provide the perfect lookout place to spot the arrival of marauding pirates which would often attack and invade

Lanzarote and specifically, Teguise. On some occasions inhabitants of Teguise would take refuge in the castle. This was mostly in vain given that this castle could offer locals little chance of victory faced with a better prepared enemy and in most cases the islanders were considerably outnumbered. Today the castle now houses the Pirate Museum which displays details of some of the pirate incursions on Lanzarote.

Pelotamano

This sport is currently only played in Teguise, Tiagua and Soo, but it is hoped that young people will be encouraged to take it up and play this traditional game before it disappears completely.

Teguise - Las Caleras and San Rafael chapel (1 kilometre)

From *calle los Árboles* street you should head north along an alley called *calle Fondaje* which opens up at a crossroads with *calle Alcornoque* and follow this route along *calle Guincho*. The asphalt path comes to an end and turns into a dirt road. Some 500 metres along you will see some stone structures to your right; these are lime kilns, you are in the Chimida limestone quarry where the limestone would be broken up ready to be placed in the kilns. The lime burners would prepare the kiln by filling it with firewood, usually made up of Mediterranean saltwort, barbed wire bush and similar tinder, and it would be their job to keep stoking the oven and ensure it continued burning for several days until the lime was produced. Lime was used in the olden days for various purposes; as mortar for construction, to paint the walls of houses and to disinfect the *aljibe* water deposits. Lime from Lanzarote was exported to other islands and parts of Africa. To the south you will see the small San Rafael church which has been a place of devotion since the beginning of the 15th century and has been remodelled many times. You can return to Teguise the same way or along *calle Iballa*.

Walk 14 — Montaña Blanca

Difficulty rating: moderate
Type: circular
Approximate distance: 8 kilometres
Approximate timing: 3 hours
Terrain gradient: 504 ▲ 504 ▲
Signposting:
There are sections marked 'GR' for long routes with white and red signs. Others are marked as short, or 'PR' routes with white and yellow stripes and others are white and green, denoting local routes.

Departure/Finishing point:
Plaza de Montaña Blanca square
UTM:
28 R6325373207341

Montaña Blanca is an ancient volcanic cone whose height of 598 metres is quite considerable when compared to the general elevation of the island. Its central location means that when you reach the summit you can enjoy spectacular views of nearly all the different landscapes on the island. The caldera and the northern face were once covered with fertile farmlands where pulses, vegetables and cereals grew. Today, the northern side together with the rest of the surrounding areas are where grapes are grown forming part of the protected landscape of La Geria.

This walk also gives hikers valuable insights into the history of the island as it takes you to some archaeological remains of the indigenous *Majos* tribes and also to a tremendous feat of human engineering designed to collect the scarce rainwater, the *maretas* of Montaña Blanca.

Walk 14

Walk description

The walk starts off in the main village square in Montaña Blanca, next to the María Auxiliadora church (building of which was finished in 1952) and the Lomo de Tesa Sociocultural Centre (built in 1978). To begin with you need to walk southwest along *calle La Degollada* - a paved path that later becomes a dirt road until reaching the narrow gorge that separates Montaña Blanca mountain and the Lomo de Tesa ridge. Halfway up there is an option to choose an alternative walk (see Alternative route for details). From here you can see the town of Tías and the Los Ajaches mountain range in the south of Lanzarote as well as the tiny island, Isla de Lobos, and Fuerteventura. Keep walking along this path which starts to descend and continue until you reach an intersection where

HOW TO GET THERE

By bus: there are regular public transport links between Arrecife and Montaña Blanca on the San Bartolomé route.
By road: the LZ-301.

POINTS OF INTEREST

- The Montaña Blanca and Guatisea archeological sites (continued overleaf)

Montaña Blanca

- The Montaña Blanca and Guatisea water reservoirs (*maretas*)
- The Protected Landscape of La Geria

you need to take the footpath to your left. Just after passing an *aljibe* with no roof and another water deposit, turn northwards towards Montaña Blanca itself. When you reach the foot of the mountain, turn eastwards and start a 20 metre descent down a volcanic ash track. The path you need is on the left and goes over a pipe that leads to the water collection reservoirs, or *maretas*, of Montaña Blanca. As you walk, you will see alongside you the archaeological remains of the *Majos*, the ancient inhabitants of the island, canals, petroglyphs, animal representations - the collection make for some enigmatic finds which archaeologists and historians are still trying to fathom, even today. Please be careful not to tread on any remains so as to avoid their deterioration.

Once you reach the *maretas* you can appreciate the immense scale of the work that was embarked upon in the 1940s in an ambitious plan to supply water to towns all the way down to Arrecife. In the end, the water could only reach as far as Tías. The southern face of the mountain serves as a natural reservoir that collects rainwater. The rainwater collects in a canal dug out of the side of the mountain and due to the downward slope, runs down into drainage tanks where the solids (stones and sand) are filtered leaving the liquid to fill the *maretas*.

Interior view of the *mareta* at Montaña Blanca.

Walk 14

ROUTE PROFILE

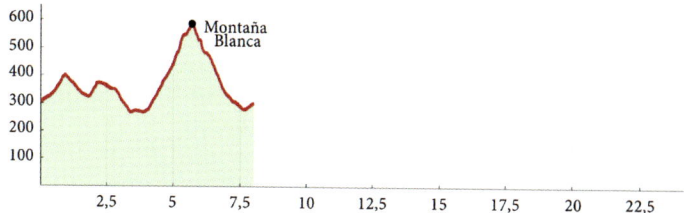

The two *maretas*, or manmade reservoirs, at Montaña Blanca are identical in size; measuring 54 metres long, 7 m high and 5 metres wide. They represent the great need to find solutions to the scarcity of natural water on the island prior to the arrival of the desalination plants in 1964. The *maretas* were abandoned in the eighties.

Back on the trail; you need to follow the path east along the track made to allow access for lorries transporting water from the *maretas*. Skirt the mountain and continue round until you reach an area with animal pens. Just here is the dirt track that will take you quite steeply up the mountain as far as the caldera, or crater's edge. To get to the summit you need to turn left towards the Pico de la Cruz peak. Look carefully to the right and you will find the path for the descent, just below a small stone shack. As you have come this far, it is worth making the effort to go all the way to the summit, though. Keep Pico de La Cruz to the left of you - this is where locals from Montaña Blanca village come in May to decorate the cross with flowers in celebration of the Day of the Cross festival before going to the caldera where they spend the day together. From here to the summit there is a simple ridge, but take care, as on extremely windy days it can make you a little unsteady at this altitude. At the top of the mountain you are 598 metres above sea level. It is well worth spending some time here to admire the sensational views and take in the panoramic vistas of practically all the island as well as Fuerteventura, Isla de Lobos, the Chinijo

LINKS WITH OTHER WALKS

- Teguise - Tías (Walk 3)

- Puerto del Carmen - Tinajo - La Santa (Walk 6)

Montaña Blanca

> 'Ever since we moved to Lanzarote I have been saying to Pilar that I would climb all those mountains at the back of my house and yesterday I made a start by taking on the highest of them all. Yesterday I climbed Montaña Blanca'
>
> **José Saramago**
> *Lanzarote Journals 1993-1995*

Archipelago and the incredible alignment of volcanoes. In the past this spot would have been used as a strategic lookout point but these days its the radio antennae that are on constant alert.

The descent takes you to the inner edge of the caldera and then snakes down to the very centre of the crater. You will see the path you came up, but there is no need to take it as it is better to take the footpath to the left in a westerly direction. This is the footpath that the farmers of yesteryear used to walk up and down in order to tend to their land. Nowadays it is used by hikers who walk in search of the most spectacular views on the island. The path then leads you to another path along the ravine and to La Degollada gorge and back to the departure point.

Alternative route

If you just wish to climb directly to the top of Montaña Blanca, you will find the path is halfway up the ascent to the La Degollada gorge, on the left next to some animal pens. This was the original footpath used by locals and their livestock to traipse up and down the mountain for their daily work on the land. The path takes you as far as the caldera and from there on head for the Pico de La Cruz peak and carry on along this ridge to the summit of the mountain. For the descent it is best to head north, zigzagging towards the inner part of the caldera and keeping an eye out for the path that you initially used that will take you back down to the village.

POINTS OF INTEREST

Montaña Blanca and Guatisea reservoirs (*maretas*)

These are huge manmade reservoirs excavated out of the interior of the mountains and in use from the 1940s until the 1960s. The southern part of these mountains has no soil, but a type of igneous volcanic rock instead, which means that the rainfall runs off the surface and is collected into a canal dug out of a lower part of the volcano. Gravity pulls the water into these drainage areas where the stone and sand mixed with the water are filtered before passing through into the *maretas* as clean drinking water. Montaña Guatisea has six such deposits and Montaña Blanca has two which are currently undergoing restoration work.

Protected Landscape of La Geria

The area of La Geria was legally declared a Protected Natural Space in 1987 and designated a Natural Park to later be reclassified in the category of Protected Landscape under the auspices of the 12/1994 Law (now D.L 1/2000). It consists of a vast area of land measuring some 5,255 hectares, all of which covered by the volcanic sand or ash that was dramatically spewed out during the eruptions at Timanfaya in the 18th century. Farmers have dug deep pits in the volcanic ash to plant vines and many of them are protected by horseshoes of volcanic rocks that offer shelter from the trade winds. This garden area of Lanzarote is like nowhere else on earth; its unique landscape is a stunning sight to behold for walkers as they venture through the footpaths. The area covers five island municipalities; Yaiza, Tías, San Bartolomé, Teguise and Tinajo. Amongst many other awards, La Geria received the award for best Cultural Landscape in the Canaries from the CICOP foundation (*International Centre for Conservation of Heritage*) and was also the only Spanish nomination for the Council of Europe's Landscape Prize.

Walk 15 — Caldera Blanca

Difficulty rating: moderate
Type: circular
Approximate distance: 11 kilometres
Approximate timing: 4 ½ hours
Terrain gradient: 466 ▲ 466 ▲
Signposting: some sections are marked as short, or 'PR' routes with white and yellow signs.

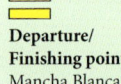

Departure/Finishing point: Mancha Blanca Cultural Centre
UTM: 28R6277223213530

This walk is a must in order to fully explore the volcanic terrain that is so characteristic of the island of Lanzarote. It provides an overview of the different landscapes of the *malpaís*, or 'badlands' created by the eruptions of the 18th century in which you can also see small rises or *islotes* which are areas of older land that are raised and have remained untouched by the volcanic eruptions around them. Caldera Blanca is a special example of this type of rise as it has a crater which measures more than a kilometre in diameter. From up high you will be able to see how the horizon is dominated by the presence of volcanic cones, vast expanses of lava flow and volcanic sand. Hikers will be afforded spectacular panoramic views of Timanfaya and a large part of Lanzarote. Caldera Blanca forms part of the Volcano Natural Park.

Walk 15

Walk description

Take the village of Mancha Blanca in the municipality of Tinajo as your departure point. Head towards the Fire Mountains along *calle Chimanfaya* street and the LZ -67. After about 150 metres you will start to leave Mancha Blanca behind you and in front of you, you will see a dirt road going west; this is the path you need and when the dirt road ends it turns into a path which takes you through the lava fields created by the Timanfaya eruptions in the 18th century. Keep heading west along the path that takes you to the Islote La Caldereta rise; remember you are walking on terrain created by volcanoes, so you can expect it to be rocky and jagged at times. Walk around the north face and you will see an opening with an *aljibe*, a few animal pens and stone huts. Keep along the path heading

HOW TO GET THERE

By bus: there are regular public transport links between Arrecife and Mancha Blanca
By road: from Arrecife on the LZ-20 then *Avenida de los Los Volcanes* avenue and *calle Chimanfaya* street.

Caldera Blanca

POINTS OF INTEREST

- The Los Volcanes Natural Park
- *Islote* rises (Kipuka)

west towards Caldera Blanca. Once at the base there are some stone pens which you should have your back to as you continue around the mountain. Approximately 40 metres on you will see the footpath that takes you up the side of the mountain to the very top of the cone. From up here you can stop and marvel at the biggest and most spectacular crater on the island which boasts a diameter of more than 1 kilometre. Keep walking on the left in order to reach the summit at 458 metres. The panoramic views from

POINTS OF INTEREST

Islote **rises (Kipuka)**

The term *islote* is used in Lanzarote to refer to a raised piece of land that is older than the land surrounding it, such as the Islote de Uga (or Huga), La Caldereta and Caldera Blanca which were surrounded by the lava flow of the 18th century. They are areas of raised terrain which the lava flow could not cover and therefore they have remained intact. Out of reach of the treacherous lava flow, they provided safe havens, to flora and fauna that did not perish or disappear under the sea of volcanic lava.

Walk 15

ROUTE PROFILE

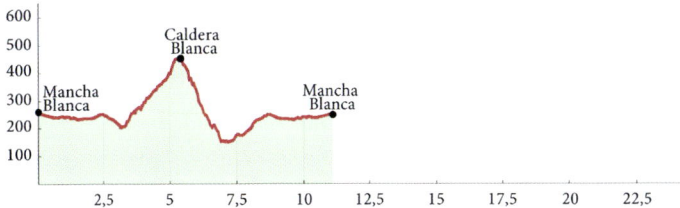

here are incredible and take in the volcanoes that erupted in the 18th century as well as the two cones that erupted in the 19th century. It is worth remembering that prior to these eruptions, there once stood villages, settlements and farmlands that were subsequently totally buried by the fury of the volcano.

Keep walking around the rim of the volcano until you face west and look out for the descending footpath. Once at the foot of the mountain, walk back round, heading east towards the path you arrived on. From here you can retrace your footsteps back to where you started. This is the end of the walk.

LINKS WITH OTHER WALKS

- Timanfaya coastline (Walk 10)

- Puerto del Carmen - Tinajo - La Santa (Walk 6)

Walk 16 — Santa Catalina

Difficulty rating: easy
Type: circular
Approximate distance: 9 kilometres
Approximate timing: 3 hours 30 minutes
Terrain gradient: 186 ▲ 186 ▼
Signposting: no signposting
Departure/Finishing point: The LZ-56 Tinguatón road
UTM: 28 R6279453212071

Suitable for families with children and users of joëlettes or specially adapted wheelchairs.

This is a spectacular walk through volcanic terrain in part of the Los Volcanes Natural Park. It takes you to the Caldera de Santa Catalina, (Caldera de la Rilla), the very mouth of the eruptions that took place in the 18th century. It is a lunar landscape filled with craters and seas of petrified lava where the land displays a myriad of hues and textures. Despite the hundreds of years that have passed, you can still see where the rivers of molten lava once bubbled and flowed from the El Señalo volcano and the Pico Partido peak. The long-buried villages remain dormant, but their presence is still palpable underfoot.

Walk 16

Walk description

This route starts by the side of the LZ-56 road at the exit of Tinguatón towards La Geria. It starts in a car park with some palm trees (*Phoenix canariensis*) between the Montaña Tabaiba/Norte and Montaña de Los Rostros mountains. Very close to here is the location of the ancient town of Mancha Blanca that was totally buried by the seas of lava that spewed forth from the mouth of the volcanoes in Timanfaya in the 18th century. Start walking southwest along a flat dirt road and take the first fork left heading south towards the Islote de Los Rodeos - a mountain that shows the scars of considerable human interference, as it has been quarried for its volcanic sand used to create artifical farmlands in other places on the island. You will start to walk around the base of the mountain heading right, towards the west

HOW TO GET THERE

- By bus: regular public transport: Arrecife - Mancha Blanca.
- By road: from Arrecife on the LZ-20, LZ-30 and LZ-56 roads

POINTS OF INTEREST

- The Los Volcanes Natural Park
- *Islote* rises (Kipuka)

163

and when you reach a fork in the path, notice that the footpath to the left starts to ascend; this will be your return path. Now, you need to take the right-hand fork that takes you on a path to an old quarry where the volcanic pebbles (*rofe*) used to be extracted. The footpath ends here and from now on you need to walk on a rougher *rofe*-covered track that heads west between fig trees. You are now walking along the edge of the Caldera de Santa Catalina. The track starts to go uphill and you will see how a native species of sorrel, (*Rumex lunaria*), has managed to colonize the terrain having evolved the capability of surviving in such an inhospitable environment. As you walk you will see the spectacular fields of lava flow and the Pico Partido and Señalo cones; a collection of eruptive mouths from which the lava flowed, totally engulfing the villages of Jarretas and Suan Juan, among others.

Once on the western face, take the track on

Walk 16

ROUTE PROFILE

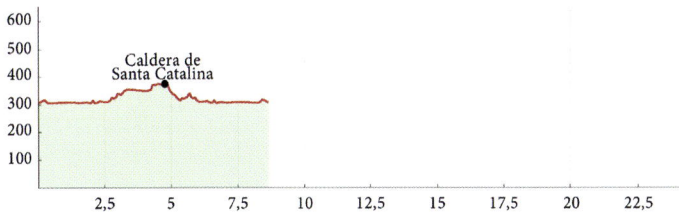

the upper ridge of the volcano which is about 20 metres ahead. When you get to the top you will see before you the impressive sight of one of the most spectacular craters on the island; it is symmetrical and its base is shattered and shaped like a fishbone; it is quite unique, this is the Caldera de Santa Catalina. Faced with the volcano's terrible might, popular legend tells of how the inhabitants of Santa Catalina calmly collected their belongings and walked to the north of the island where they established the village of Los Valles. On 7th September 1730, just seven days after the start of the eruptions, the original town of Santa Catalina and that of Maretas were completely buried under the lava flow.

It is best not to go any further into the caldera nor walk around its rim so as not to damage the fragile landscape or disturb the peace and quiet of a Barbary falcon (*Falco pelegrinoides*) that might be nesting in the region. The return journey is back along the same path but this time south first, and then east. The lava fields extend towards the mountains in La Geria and as far as the distant towns of Uga and Yaiza which were also affected by the eruptions in Timanfaya to a certain extent. When you get to the east of the caldera, keep heading east to get to the Islote de Los Rodeos. You will get to some dirt tracks where you should take the left turn, walking downhill until you get to the road you came up at the beginning of the walk. The return leg now is the same way back to the car park beside the LZ-56. You have completed the walk.

LINKS WITH OTHER WALKS

- Caldera de los Cuervos and Montaña Colorada (Walk 17)

- Caldera Blanca (Walk 15)

- Puerto del Carmen - Tinajo - La Santa (Walk 6)

Walk 17 — Caldera de los Cuervos and Montaña Colorada

Difficulty rating: easy
Type: circular
Approximate distance: 7 kilometres
Approximate timing: 2 hours 30 minutes
Terrain gradient: 150 / ▲ 145 ▲
Signposting: no signposting. Information boards provide details about the volcanic landscape.
Departure/Finishing point: The LZ-56 Tinguatón road next to the Caldera de los Cuervos
UTM: 28 R6280973207897

This is a walk which embraces one of the most important aspects of Lanzarote's history as it takes you to the very place where the eruptions that were to change the course of the island's history both started and finished. This route gives you the chance to see the two volcanoes where it all began; the spectacular Caldera de los Cuervos where the Timanfaya cycle of eruptions started that fateful day on 1st September 1730, and Montaña Colorada, the volcano that drew this period of eruptions to a close with its sea of lava that stopped just as it reached the entrance to Tinajo in April 1735.

This route takes you on a journey through time as you walk over vast fields of solidified lava and remember the towns of Chimanfaya, Guimón, Candelaria (or Masintafe) that lie buried underfoot, and the legend of Virgen de los Dolores (Our Lady of Sorrows). It truly is a unique walk that takes you through a stunning landscape replete with geological marvels in the heart of the Los Volcanes Natural Park.

Walk 17

Walk description

Caldera de Los Cuervos

The best place to start this walk is on the LZ-56 road at Tinguatón where the municipality of Tías ends and Tinajo begins. To one side of you stands the Caldera de Los Cuervos (a.k.a Caldera de Las Lapas) and on the other side is Montaña Negra and to the northeast with its unmistakable red hues, is the Montaña Colorada mountain. The parish priest of Yaiza wrote in his diary of how the most important eruptions in the Canary Islands in the last 500 years began; '*On the first day of September 1730, between nine and ten o'clock at night, the earth suddenly broke open near Chimanfaya, two leagues away from Yaiza. That first night an enormous mountain reared up from the belly of the earth and from its peak,*

HOW TO GET THERE

There are no public transport links.
By road: from Arrecife on the LZ-20, LZ-30 and LZ-56 roads.

POINTS OF INTEREST

- The Los Volcanes Natural Park

167

Caldera de los Cuervos and Montaña Colorada

The logo of Lanzarote designed by César Manrique was inspired by the island's volcanic history and depicts an erupting volcano. .

flames leapt and burned incessantly for nineteen days.' This mountain described by the priest stands to the west; the Caldera de Los Cuervos.

Your walk towards this caldera begins here at the boundaries of the two municipalities. It is a path covered with *lapilli* (the tephra or coarse volcanic ash pebbles ejected by volcanoes) and takes you on a gentle route all the way to the foot of the volcano which you are going to climb heading north to the right. A few metres ahead to your left you will see an opening which is too inviting to resist. Assuming you have succumbed to temptation, climb down into the centre of the crater where the silence provides the perfect moment for quiet contemplation as you immerse yourself in the sight and sound of this magnificent natural auditorium that lies protected by its jagged upper ridges.

The orange colours around the caves are due to the presence of nitrophilous lichen (*Xantoria sp.*) which rely on nitrates to survive and which they obtain from bird excrement. The Canary sorell (*Rumex lunaria*) and the rose geranium (*Pelargonium capitatum*) are the two most visible plant species in the crater. Exit the same way as you entered and continue to climb the cone westwards, you can see the Fire Mountains in the distance in Timanfaya National Park. During the climb you will observe areas where the *lapilli* has been quarried for use in the construction of tourist complexes on the island in the 1970s and 80s. Once at the east face of the mountain, you can marvel at the views before returning down the same route to the departure point.

Walk 17

ROUTE PROFILE

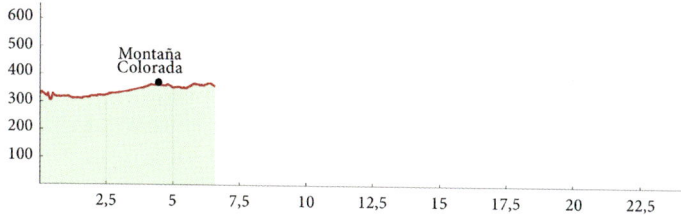

Caldera de los Cuervos - Montaña Colorada

LINKS WITH OTHER WALKS

- Santa Catalina (Walk 16)

You can get close to Montaña Colorada by car on the LZ-56 road as there is a good place to park just one and a half kilometres further on the right. You can also walk there by crossing the road and heading east towards a small stone house at the base of Montaña Negra. When you get to Montaña Negra, you will see there is water in its interior, this is the Montaña Negra spring. This spring captures the water that runs down the side of this old mountain which was covered with volcanic sand by the eruptions of the 18th century. The layer of volcanic *rofe* pebbles (*lapilli* /volcanic ash) retains the night's humidity as well as the scarce rainfall water and filters it into the interior layers of the mountain where gravity takes care of carrying the water down into pools where it collects naturally. The ancient inhabitants were the first to notice these natural seepages so they built a receptacle to store the water and this is what you can now see. Follow the *rofe* path north until you reach Montaña Colorada.

Montaña Colorada

This is the volcano which was about to engulf the village of Tinajo in 1735, when the locals famously came out in procession carrying the statue of the Virgen de Los Dolores (Our Lady of Sorrows), and in response the sea of molten lava came to a miraculous halt. The chapel was built in her honour years later (see page 101). This route

Caldera de los Cuervos and Montaña Colorada

takes you all the way around the volcano, firstly heading east where a blanket of green and white lichen covers part of the landscape. You will also see here at the easternmost point an enormous ball of basalt rock some 30 metres away. Its round shape would seem to indicate that it is a volcanic bomb, that is to say a piece of lava ejected by the volcano.

POINTS OF INTEREST

The Los Volcanes Natural Park

This area was initially declared a Protected Natural Space in accordance with the 12/1987 law and designated a Natural Park together with La Geria. It was later reclassified in 1994 when it was designated a Volcanic Natural Park by the 12/1994 law which was subsequently subsumed by Decree-Law 1/2000. It has a surface area of 10,158 hectares that extends over the municipalities of Tinajo, Yaiza and Tías. It is a landscape of volcanic cones and lava flows that date back to the sequence of eruptions in Timanfaya in 18th century and also the eruption of Tinguatón Volcano in 1824. It is a territory with ancient rises (Kipukas) and unique geological formations and it also includes the fishing village of El Golfo in its boundaries. It is a truly awe-inspiring landscape that surrounds Timanfaya National Park.

Its sheer size is quite astounding and makes you wonder exactly how it was formed. One theory is that its round shape was acquired as it cooled down while spinning in the air before landing. All around you is a vast field of solidified lava which buried several villages; Gumón, Candelaria, Tomaren, Masintafe, Masdache and Mozaga. As you keep walking around the northern face of the cone you can see how it looks like it has been eaten away. This is because its sand and gravel were quarried for use elsewhere on the island - an unfortunate example of human ignorance at not knowing to choose an alternative site that would have had less impact on the landscape. Looking north, you can see an old volcano called Montaña Ortiz, it is a rare sight made rather unusual because of the asymmetry of its eastern face whereas the majority of volcanoes on Lanzarote are asymmetrical on the northern face as this is the direction from which the prevailing trade winds blow. Keep hiking on and you will see how the lava flow twisted and swirled as it gushed down from the crater, an image that has been captured for eternity as the molten lava solidified. As you look west, the Las Nueces cone is close by. This is the volcano responsible for spewing a vast sea of lava that reached as far as Arrecife. Just a few metres on you will see the Montaña Colorada car park. If you left your vehicle in the car park next to the Caldera de Los Cuervos, you simply need to retrace your steps heading south. You have reacehd the end of the route.

Ramalina Strap lichen (*Ramalina bourgeana*): It is a dye-producing lichen much used by islanders. Together with variegated foam lichen (*Sterocaulon vesuvianum*) they are the two most abundant species of lichen found in the Volcanic Natural Park.

Alternative route

An alternative walk from the Montaña Negra spring is to head south and walk all the way round this old mountain itself. It is a walk which invites you to see vegetation such as mastic trees, guayaba trees, fig trees and olive trees. When you reach the north face, after passing the last of the olive trees, you will see to your right a path that takes you directly to the volcanic bomb at Montaña Colorada.

Walk 18 — La Geria

Difficulty rating: easy
Type: circular
Approximate distance: 9 kilometres
Approximate timing: 3 hours
Terrain gradient: 321 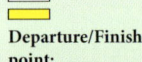 320
Signposting: Some tracks are marked with the white and red 'PR'/ short route way marks.

Departure/Finishing point: The Caridad chapel, La Geria (LZ-30)
UTM: 28 R6252783205227

La Geria is Lanzarote's unique vineyard. It is an area that holds a fascinating beauty and a wealth of ethnographic riches. The region has been transformed by the ingenious touch of man who has managed to plant crops and eke out a living from this barren landscape after the devastating volcanic eruptions of Timanfaya. Vast fields of *lapilli* - or volcanic pebble ash covered the valley of La Geria, engulfing the fields of cereal plantations that had once flourished there. Farmers dug out each individual pit, one by one, where they planted grape vines (*Vitis vinifera*) and other fruit trees like fig trees (*Ficus carica*) and black mulberry bushes (*Morus nigra*). Each vine would have to be nurtured by hand, with the grape growers traipsing up and down to each pit to prune, dig, treat and harvest the grapes. Once the grapes have been picked the wine producers start the process of making the wines. The end result can be tasted in the various wineries, or *bodegas*, that have been established in La Geria.

Walk 18

Walk description

The starting point for this walk is the 18th century La Caridad chapel just next to the LZ-30 road and the wineries of La Geria and Rubicón. The chapel predates the eruptions and although untouched by the molten lava flow it was buried under layers of volcanic lapilli. Walk parallel to the LZ-30 road for about 70 metres and take the dirt road left, heading west. The walk takes you through a vast landscape that is almost other worldly in appearance. The footpaths lead you through lands dotted with pits which have been hand-dug especially for the precious vines to grow within. The main grape varieties in this region are the white listan and the volcanic malvasia grape. To the right you will see a fork, here you need to take the track heading north walking past the flanks of Montaña Diama. You

HOW TO GET THERE:

There are no public transport links.
By road: from Arrecife on the LZ-20 and then the LZ-30 roads.

POINT OF INTEREST

- The Diama archaeological site in La Geria
(continued overleaf)

La Geria

- La Caridad chapel
- The Guardilama canals
- Protected Landscape of La Geria

LINKS WITH OTHER WALKS

-Yaiza - Playa Blanca (Walk 5)

-Playa Blanca - Janubio (Walk 9)

will pass a group of houses nicknamed 'the old cemetery' where you can see some *aljibe* water deposits that have stood the test of time and have survived being buried under layers of volcanic lapilli pebbles before being uncovered. At the junction here you need to take the path going left which continues around Montaña Diama. Look out for the palm tree to the north with the dried out trunk of another palm tree. As you hike on you should now go east, to the right which takes you to the LZ-30 road that runs through the centre of the island. Once at the main road, turn right and carefully walk along the verge by the side of the road which passes a small *bodega* which is worth popping into to sample its homemade wine (see alternative route 1). When you're ready, keep walking until you come to the first dirt road on the left which heads south (*the Camino de Bilbao*). This track leads you to a private house, but there is no need to walk that far, as approximately 300 metres further on you will need to take a left turn going east along a narrower footpath between vines and their pits.

POINTS OF INTEREST

La Caridad Chapel

The chapel was built in the 17th century in the heart of La Geria estate; this was land that belonged to the archpriest, Diego de Laguna. It houses a picture of Our Lady of Charity - Caridad - whose Saint's day falls on 15th August which coincides with the grape harvest. This building pre-dates the volcanic eruptions of the 18th century and during this period it was covered with volcanic ash and *lapilli*.

Walk 18

ROUTE PROFILE

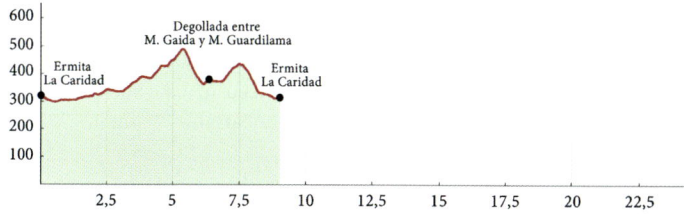

You will soon come to another dirt track with two possible directions; you should take the right-hand path which climbs up in a south-easterly direction towards the Montaña Gaida, which is completely covered with volcanic *lapilli* ash and vines.

Approximately half way up this path is the head of the Obispo gully that has a permanent source of freshwater which comes from the dew that falls at night and the occasional rainfall that is captured and filtered through the volcanic ash. There is another junction in the path here; go left towards the south. The right-hand fork takes you all the way up to the summit of Montaña Guardilama if you wish to have a detour (see alternative route 2). But to continue this trail you will see that the ascent ends in the narrow gorge (*degollada*) which separates Montaña Gaida from Mt. Guardilama. Walk down a loose pebble-strewn track that takes you to La Asomada. After a while you will reach the La Caldereta trail which you need to join by turning right in a westerly direction. At the top of the climb there is a crossroads; the path straight opposite is the El Tablero trail that takes you to the village of Uga (see Walk 4); to the left you have Montaña Tinasoria and to the right, Mt. Guardilama. Take the right-hand trail and walk some 250 metres around the edge of a vineyard (see alternative route 2). Now the path starts to descend, turn left and look for a narrow footpath that heads northwest between vines and Spanish cane (*Arundo donax*). You will pass a huge palm

> **Lanzarote: Its wines, landscapes and culture**
>
> This book, written by Rubén Acosta and Mario Ferrer, provides a guide to the wine growing culture of the island through its history, natural and social values and from an oenological perspective. Apart from offering practical information, the guide also invites readers to discover the landscape of La Geria and to find out all about the wines produced in Lanzarote.
>
>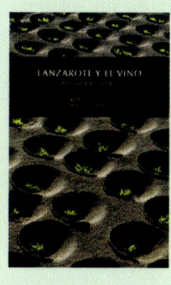

La Geria

WHAT TO VISIT

- The Bodega Rubicón winery
- The Bodega La Geria winery
- The Bodega Stratvs winery
- The El Chupadero winery
- The Bodega Diama winery

tree that has another spring at its base which was very important in the past owing to the scarcity of water on the island. Continue your descent and look out for some large specimens of Canary sorrel (*Rumex lunaria*), barbed-wire bushes (*Launaea arborescens*) and Lanzarote trefoil lotus (*Lotus lancerottensis*) and common white saladillo (*Polycarpaea nivea*). The trail opens out into a wider path here. Keep going north and then you will pass the *bar-bodega* El Chupadero where the dirt road takes you to the LZ-30 in no time. Turn left and you will see the La Caridad chapel once more and you can round off the walk in one of the nearby *bodegas* with a refreshing glass of malvasia wine.

Alternative route 1: Heart of La Geria

Once on the LZ-30 road you can walk along the verge on the left-hand side heading southwest towards the La Caridad chapel, past the Bodega Stratvs and Bodega Diama wineries.

Alternative route 2: La Geria and Montaña Guardilama

Once on the upper rim of Montaña Guardilama's caldera you have the option of going left and continuing to climb the mountain to its summit at 603 m. The peak offers magnificent views of La Geria, the volcanoes and the south of Lanzarote as well as its surrounding islands, Fuerteventura, Isla de Lobos, and the smaller islets in the north of Lanzarote.

The trail going back down is quite steep and can be slippery, so you should take the descent with great care. Some 250 metres before reaching the Caldereta, or Tinasoria path, you will find the footpath that descends on the right, heading northwest. You are now back on Walk 18.

ALTERNATIVE 1

Difficulty rating: easy
Type: circular
Approximate distance: 4 kilometres
Approximate timing: 1 hour
Suitable for families with children and users of joëlettes or specially adapted wheelchairs.

ALTERNATIVE 2

Difficulty: advanced
Type: circular
Approximate distance: 8 kilometres
Approximate timing: 3 hours

The Diama Archaeological site in La Geria
As layers of volcanic sand (*rofe*) have gradually been removed, it has revealed the remains of structures such as *aljibe* water deposits, walls etc. that stood long before the onslaught of the volcanic eruptions. Some of these archaeologically important remains can be found at this site in the northern part of the La Geria valley.

The Guardilama Canals
At the northwest rim of the Guardilama caldera they have excavated a series of canals that had been dug in the basalt rock by the *Majos*, the ancient inhabitants of the island. Visitors are asked to be careful as they move around the site out of respect for the island's historical heritage.

Protected Landscape of La Geria
The area of La Geria was legally declared a Protected Natural Space in accordance with the 12/1987 Law and designated a Natural Park to be reclassified later in the category of Protected Landscape by the 12/1994 Law and subsequently Decree-Law 1/2000. It consists of a huge area of land measuring some 5,255 hectares and covers five island municipalities; Yaiza, Tías, Tinajo, San Bartolomé and Teguise. The landscape is dominated by the dramatic pits and hollows dedicated to growing vines under a protective layer of volcanic pebbles (*rofe*) and sheltered by low semi-circular walls made of volcanic rocks.

Walk 19 — The Pico Redondo Peak - Femés

Difficulty rating: moderate
Type: circular
Approximate distance: 6 kilometres
Approximate timing: 2 hours 30 minutes.
Terrain gradient: 402 402
Signposting: Some tracks are marked with the white and red stripes denoting a 'PR', or short route and others parts are way-marked with orange dots.

Departure/Finishing point: Plaza de Femés square
UTM: 28 R6189743198965

This walks offers the chance to trek through the Los Ajaches mountains which were formed approximately 14 million years ago, making it the oldest mountain range on Lanzarote and the first part of the island to have surged up through the sea. This is a landscape characterised by its expansive hillsides, wide open valleys and a multitude of surface dykes which show deep erosion processes that provide a good indication as to the sheer age of the region.

Throughout the island's history, this has been an area dedicated to livestock farming, and indeed, this is still the case today all over the region. The walk through this dry sterile terrain rewards hikers with impressive panoramas and the walk around the Pico Redondo peak helps you get a real sense of the island itself and its different landscapes.

Walk 19

Femés

(Map showing route around Pico Redondo 551, Iglesia de San Marcial, LZ 702)

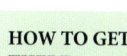

Walk description

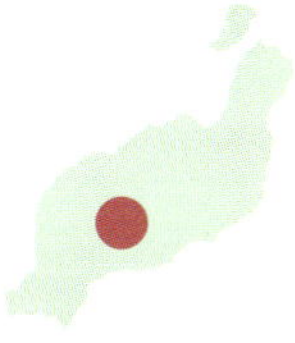

The village of Femés peers over the southern flatlands like a balcony perched on top of one of the area's peaks. Femés was the former capital of the municipality until 1952. The walk starts in the village square where the 18th century San Marcial church stands. It is the legacy of the first San Marcial cathedral which originally stood on the beaches of Papagayo in the city of Rubicón founded in 1404 by Jean de Bethencourt. The historical Papal bull of Pope Benedict XIII, dated 1404, decreed that the first diocese in the Canaries should be established there and that it was to be called Rubiscense.

On the other side of the Femés plaza is the Casa del Romero building that at one time housed pilgrims who would flock to San Marcial out of devotion and to fulfil their pledges to the

HOW TO GET THERE

By bus: there are regular public transport links between Arrecife and Femés.
By road: from Arrecife on the LZ-2 and LZ-702.

POINTS OF INTEREST

- The Los Ajaches Natural Monument (continued overleaf)

179

The Pico Redondo Peak - Femés

- The San Marcial Church
- Femés
- The Cueva Paloma Site
- The novel *Mararía*

WHERE TO VISIT

- The Quesería Rubicón cheese maker's

saint. To start the walk you need to head south, walking up a dirt road as far as a goat pen. From here you will see the vast Higueral valley below that opens out into the Playa del Pozo beach, just a few kilometres away from the small coastal hamlet of Playa Quemada. The path you need is on the right; walk past a water deposit then turn left along a narrow footpath that takes you across the so-called La Aceituna peak. This area is full of basalt dykes which are like interior veins of rock which have come to the surface due to erosion. These rocky outcrops were the result of magma trying to explode through the surface of the earth. This zone is called Riscos Bonitos, or 'pretty cliffs'. The vegetation here is long suffering and damaged by the constant to-ing and fro-ing of goats but you can see how some vegetation endeavours to hold fast, including; sea thorn (*Lycium intricatum)*, tree tobacco (*Nicotiana Glauca)*, prickle-leaved, or bitter, spurge (*Euphorbia regis-jubae*), prickly pear cactus (*Opuntia dillenii*), African foxtail grass (*Cenchrus ciliaris*) etc. When you reach the Degollada de Carlos gorge, take a moment to admire the incredible vista of the plains below including the nearby village of Maciot, the tourist resort of Playa Blanca, Fuerteventura just beyond and also the small Isla de Lobos. The footpath continues south covered with a layer of yellow-coloured volcanic stones. The path forks in two

Walk 19

ROUTE PROFILE

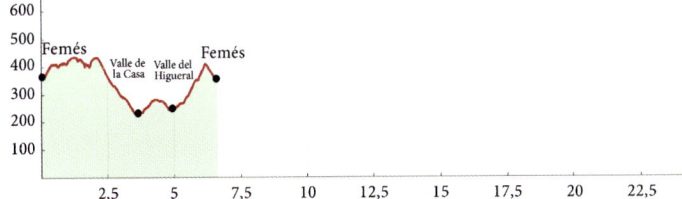

near the next gorge, the Degollada del Portugués. Take the left fork which climbs up to the Morro de los Dises headland. From high up here you can see the La Casa gulley that lies to the left and the Dises gulley to the right. You can clearly see the walls of the manmade terraces which suggest that this land was once cultivated. The path starts to zigzag down now and to the right you can see the Ajache Grande (called Hacha Grande ('large axe' by some) which is the highest peak in this region. You will then reach a wooden way-marker with an orange dot which points to the left northwards. You need to climb down to the bottom of the La Casa gully ready to cross to the other side and start the ascent. Walk past a stone outhouse and an *aljibe* water deposit that collects rainwater and would have been used by farmers in the olden days to supply drinking water for their animals.

Keep hiking north until you reach the Higueral valley. The path continues northwest, and if you look up high, you can catch a glimpse of the goat pens that will just about be visible by now - they are your goal, albeit a tricky one. When you get to the bottom of the gully and see a fork on the path, take the left turn and continue your ascent up towards the goat pens. The final kilometre is hard-going and is bound to bring out a sweat but will be well worth the effort once you have reached El Filo, as the area where the pens are located is called. All you need do now is catch your breath, enjoy the views and when you are ready, begin your descent back down to Femés where you first started your hike through the Los Ajaches massif.

LINKS WITH OTHER WALKS

- Yaiza - Playa Blanca (Walk 5)

- Papagayo (Walk 20)

The Pico Redondo Peak - Femés

POINTS OF INTEREST

The San Marcial Church

The creation of the San Marcial church is inextricably linked to the conquest of Lanzarote by the Normans Jean de Bethencourt and Gadifer de La Salle who built the first church in honour of San Marcial on the beaches of Papagayo. It was declared a cathedral on 7th July 1404 in accordance with the Papal bull issued by Pope Benedict XIII. Thus, the first diocese in the whole of the Canaries was founded; the diocese of *Rubiscense*. It took its name from *Rubicón*, the name given to the fortification built at the time of the conquest and which was declared a city in compliance with the same Papal bull. San Marcial is the patron saint of Lanzarote and July 7th commemorates this important day in the island's religious history. When the conquest of Gran Canaria came to an end, the diocese was relocated to the Santa Ana cathedral in Las Palmas and the diocese was renamed the 'Canarian Diocese of Rubiscense'. The original Rubicón church was moved to Femés in order to guard it against pirate attacks on the coast in the 17th century and it was reconstructed as the Iglesia de San Marcial church in 1730.

Walk 19

Femés

The village of Femés has historically been linked to agriculture and livestock farming. It is located in the head of the valley of the same name and has a sedimentary basin with fertile topsoil. This proved ideal for planting cereals in the past and currently it is where vegetables, legumes, potatoes and other crops are cultivated. Livestock was, and still remains, the engine that has driven the region's economy together with the more recent addition of goat's cheese production. Femés is home to the San Marcial church built in honour of the patron saint of the island and is the focus point of devotion for the many pilgrims who regularly flock there. Femés was an independent municipality up until 1952 when it merged with Yaiza. It has a population of approximately 300 inhabitants.

Mararía, by Rafael Arozarena

Is a novel written by Tenerife-born author Rafael Arozarena and published in 1973. The novel was inspired by his time spent in the village when he worked for a telephone company there. The writer draws a parallel between the main character, Mararía, and the island: a woman of great beauty whose stunning looks are at once spectacular yet tragic, her dark eyes and unique appeal prove irresistible to men. The book has been translated into several different languages and was brought to the big screen in 1998 with a film of the same name directed by Antonio Betancor.

Cueva Paloma Site

A number of archaeological sites of prime importance can be found near Femés; these include Castillejo, La Degollada, Maciot, Piedra Hincada, Morro Cañón and Peña del Guanche. The art and writings of the *Majos* are represented in many places around here, especially in the Cueva Paloma site where many different spectacular ancient motifs have been discovered.

Walk 20 — Papagayo

Difficulty rating: easy
Type: circular
Approximate distance: 7.5 kilometres
Approximate timing: 2½ hours
Terrain gradient: 207 ▲ 207 ▼
Signposting: Some tracks are marked as a heritage trail and others as the green and white local trail.

Departure/Finishing point: The last hotel in the east of Playa Blanca
UTM: 28 R6173023193130

Suitable for families with children.

This walk is ideal for those who wish to spend a day on the coast enjoying the paradise beaches of Papagayo, surrounded by crystal clear waters and protected by the mountains of the Natural Monument of the Los Ajaches massif. As well as giving you the opportunity to swim and enjoy the stunning views over to the neighbouring island of Fuerteventura and the islet Isla de Lobos, this walk also gives you the chance to learn more about the history of the island.

The southeastern tip of the island has its place in the history books due to its connection with the conquest of Lanzarote; it is where Rubicón, the first city in the Canaries was built, and also where Rubicense, the first diocese in the islands was established with its San Marcial cathedral.

Walk 20

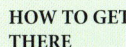

Playa Mujeres

Playa de los Pozos

Camping

Papagayo ⭐

0   0,3   0,6   0,9 km.

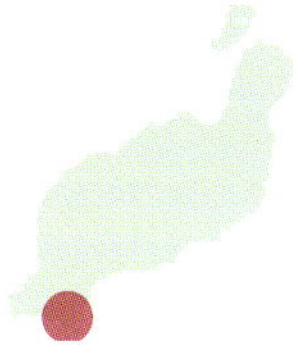

Walk description

The starting point for this walk is the very last building (a rather large hotel) to the east of the long tourist coast in the resort of Playa Blanca. Head for the path that is signposted to the beaches of Papagayo. You are now entering the Protected Natural Area of the Natural Monument of Los Ajaches. The name refers to the huge mountainous massif that stands to the north and which is the oldest territory on the island, dating back some 14 million years. The footpath takes you east and to the first beach. As you approach you will see that there are a number of different routes down to choose from, they vary in difficulty with some that are quite steep, so choose whichever path you feel up to tackling. In the first part of the Playa Mujeres beach you can see a lime kiln (*calera*) on the right which at one time gave its name to the beach as

HOW TO GET THERE

By bus: there are regular public transport links between Arrecife and Playa Blanca
By road: from Arrecife on the LZ-2.

POINTS OF INTEREST

- The Los Ajaches Natural Monument
- The City of Rubicón

Papagayo

it was previously called Playa de La Calera. Lime production was a boom industry in the past as it was a vital component in construction and from its position here next to the sea it was easily exported. You will also see a defensive machine-gun nest which has long since been abandoned and dates back to the Second World War (1939-1945). This fortification was built as a preventative measure to guard against enemy landings and raids.

Keep walking east along the beach and you will see a lone palm tree whose survival here is a clue to the presence of freshwater in the subsoil. As you leave the beach there are various different species of *psammophilus*, or sand-growing vegetation, worth noting; European searocket (*Cakile maritima*), Canary restharrow (*Ononis hesperia*), African foxtail grass (*Cenchrus ciliarus*), cup and saucer plant (*Androcymbium psamophilum*), barbed-wire bush (*Launaea arborescens*), common white saladillo (*Polycarpaea nivea*) and many more.

As the walk continues it takes you to the Los Pozos gully where you will see some walled structures with bars protecting some water wells. This is also the archaeological site of Los Pozos de San Marcial del Rubicón (see page 189). This is the spot where the Norman conquerors, Bethencourt and La Salle set up camp and built a fortress as their headquarters where they plotted how to

Walk 20

ROUTE PROFILE

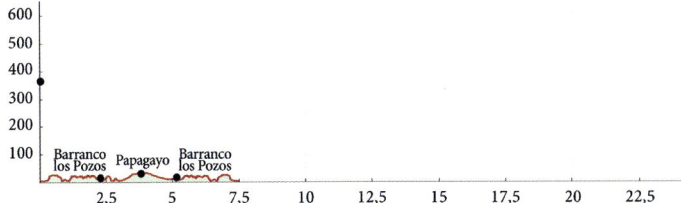

conquer the island. It is thought that the location of this site with access to a freshwater source was no fortuitous coincidence, but rather thanks to the prior knowledge of two local translators. It was also ideally situated as it was a natural port that could keep the ships in safe harbour as they set about achieving Bethencourt's plan of conquering the rest of the Canary Islands. The origin of the wells is still the subject of some debate as it has yet to be established whether they were engineered by the Normans or if they predate this period. The wellhead to raise the water and the cleaning ramp look like structures that were typical of the Carthaginian, Phoenician and Roman eras. On the interior of the Pozo de la Cruz well there are examples of rock carvings like podomorphs, and linear motifs which certainly look like they were the creations of the island's ancient indigenous civilisation. One of the images depicts a human-like figure which historians have identified as the mythological Punic goddess Tanit who was also deified by the Berber peoples in North Africa.

Approximately four metres to the east, on a small ridge, you will see a rectangular block painted white where, until a few years ago you could still see a cross; this marked the site where the first San Marcial church once stood and where on 7th July 1404, Rubiscense, the first diocese in the Canaries was established. The church was destroyed by English pirates in the 16th century and rebuilt in the village of Femés, safely inland later in the 17th century.

This city was named 'Ciudad del Rubicón', but it is not known whether this name was inspired by the ruby-red hues of the upper ridge of the gully and lands in the region, or whether it was in reference to the expression 'crossing the Rubicon',

LINKS WITH OTHER WALKS

- Yaiza - Playa Blanca (Walk 5)

- Playa Blanca - Janubio (Walk 9)

Papagayo

meaning 'reaching the point of no return' based on the phrase 'the die is cast' allegedly uttered by Julius Casear in 49 B.C. when he crossed the Italian Rubicón river and in doing so, knowingly started a war. This analogy might refer to the fact that Bethencourt and Gadifer invested their money in conquering the Canarian archipelago despite knowing it was a risky enterprise.

Back to the trek; walk along the bottom of the gully and you will see more modern wells. The water table is very close in the proximities to the coast and therefore these are not as deep as the wells in the interior of the gully. As you reach the end of the gully, walk up a path to the Papagayo beaches. Once on this footpath, turn right southwards and take the left fork at the next junction towards the Papagayo campsite. At the moment this campsite is only open in the summer months. There are two sandy coves here; Congrio beach and Puerto Muelas beach, both of which are ideal for a quick refreshing dip. Climb up a track to the south and then turn westwards to get to Papagayo beach where the old houses have been turned into bars. It truly is an idyllic location; the picturesque beach lies before you with its crystal clear waters inviting you in for a refreshing swim. To get back to the starting point for this walk, you need to follow the path west and back to the Los Pozos de San Marcial archaeological site and then head back to Playa Blanca.

Walk 20

POINTS OF INTEREST

Natural Monument of Los Ajaches

This area in the southeast of the island is a Protected Natural Space and became a designated Landscape of National Interest in accordance with the 12/1987 Law and was was later reclassified as a Natural Monument under law 12/94 subsequently subsumed by Decree-Law 1/2000. It is located in the municipality of Yaiza and encompasses the Los Ajaches mountain range, its valleys and the flatlands in the southeast of the island. In total it covers 3,009 hectares. The massif emerged from the sea some 14 million years ago, making it the oldest formation in Lanzarote. It consists of open valleys, superficial dykes, raised beaches and also boasts important archaeological and paleontological sites located in the Cueva Paloma cave, Peña del Guanche crag and the Barranco de la Pilas gulley.

The City of Rubicón

Rubicón was the first city to be established in the Canaries and was built on the site of the base camp set up by the island's Norman invaders and conquerors, Jean de Bethencourt and Gadifer de La Salle. On 7th July 1404 the Rubicón diocese was established in the San Marcial church built by Jean de Bethencourt on the beaches of Papagayo. The Rubicón settlement saw many historical events take place, such as the signing of pacts with the *Majos*, the native inhabitants of the island, the baptism and conversion to Christianity of the indigenous king Guadarfía and his subjects; and later it was the very place where he was to be captured in the infamous betrayal of Afche when Bertín de Berneval also double crossed Bethencourt and La Salle.

Rubicón

In this very place on 7th July 1404, Pope Benedict XIII founded the Diocese of Rubicón whose cathedral was built in honour of San Marcial.

This commemorative plaque was placed here on 7th July 2004 to celebrate the 6th centenary of the founding of the *Canariense-Rubicense* Diocese and the city of San Marcial.

Walk 21 — The island of La Graciosa

Difficulty rating: moderate
Type: circular
Approximate distance: 17 kilometres
Approximate timing: 5 hours 30 minutes
Terrain gradient: 146 146
Signposting: none
Departure/Finishing point: The Caleta de Sebo harbour
UTM: 28 R6455223234382

Suitable for families with children

La Graciosa is the eighth inhabited island in the Canarian archipelago and is synonymous with peace and quiet and natural beauty. Its twenty even square kilometres have been compared to a small piece of paradise that boasts a family-friendly atmosphere and a long fishing tradition.

This walk aims to unveil more about the island's history and geography and help you really get to know its idiosyncrasies through hands on contact with its protected landscape. You will have the chance to explore Caleta de Sebo and Pedro Barba, the only two residential areas of La Graciosa, as well as walk along the island's golden sandy beaches and explore its unique landscapes.

Walk 21

La Graciosa

Walk description

In order to get to La Graciosa you need to catch a ferry from the harbour in Órzola at the northernmost point of Lanzarote. The crossing to the Canaries' eighth island takes just 30 minutes.

La Graciosa has been permanently inhabited since the end of the 19th century. The first inhabitants arrived as part of a project to set up fish salting factories. This enterprise never took off, however, but the workers remained. Today the island still lives from the fishing industry, but also from tourism too as many visitors are attracted by the chance to spend some of their holiday on an island free of cars and with absolutely no asphalted roads.

The walk starts in the Caleta del Sebo harbour, the capital of the island, and heads east. You will see straight away that, indeed, none of

HOW TO GET THERE

By ferry: from the harbour in Órzola there are regular ferry crossings to the island of La Graciosa.

POINTS OF INTEREST

- The Chinijo Archipelago National Park
- La Graciosa island
- Pedro Barba
- Marine Reserve

191

The island of La Graciosa

> 'It is ten o'clock and the sun is bronzing (...), where the women climb up, laden with sacks of salted fish.'
>
> from 'Parte de una historia' by **Ignacio Aldecoa**.

the streets are tarmacked, a unique characteristic of the island which makes it particularly appealing to walkers. Pass the Nuestra Señora del Carmen church (1945), named in honour of Our Lady of Carmen, the patron saint of sailors. You will see some *aljibe* water deposits as you walk - they were an essential part of life on the island until recent years as there are no natural sources of drinking water. The path then takes you out of town heading northeast along the coast on a dusty track covered with coarse white *jable* sand. It is an area covered with white sands and coastal vegetation, including European searocket (*Cakile maritima*), Mediterranean saltwort (*Suaeda sp.*), Canary sea fennel (*Astydamia latifolia*), (*Tetraena fontanesii*) bunge, and sea spurge (*Euphorbia paralias*).

Curiously, you will also see countless numbers of *barrilitos* underfoot, these are fossils of Anthophora bees that used to live in wetlands which would suggest that at one time in the distant past the island had water. As you walk along this trail you can admire the view across to the cliffs of Famara on Lanzarote on the other side of the strait and the Punta Fariones lighthouse at the most northern tip of Lanzarote. The path continues to snake along the coastline across and around rock pools with their fascinating plant life and sea life; fish, crustaceans and seaweeds. You

Playa de las Conchas beach with views over to the island of Montaña Clara.

Walk 21

ROUTE PROFILE

will soon pass the only ravine on the island; the Barranco de los Conejos which has an attractive little beach at its mouth. The trail continues to wind around the coastline but becomes narrow and rocky underfoot until you reach Pedro Barba, La Graciosa's second residential area. It was established in the 1930s when families moved over from Lanzarote. By the 1960s when there were approximately 100 people living there, the majority sold up and either moved to Caleta del Sebo or back to Lanzarote.

With its unrivalled peace and quiet, the bay here in Pedro Barba is an ideal spot for a swim. As you wander through, you can also see how some of the inhabitants have used huge whale bones to decorate their gardens. You can leave Pedro Barba along a dirt road that heads north. Just a few metres further on you are given two options to choose from at a fork in the road; the track straight ahead takes you on Alternative route 1, but for the moment, turn right still heading north to get to Playa Lambra, (a.k.a Ambar) beach. The sandy *jable* track hugs the coast until you reach another fork where you take the right turn to the west to get to the southern face of Montaña Bermeja. As you walk further on, the trail crosses with another path which you should then take heading north by turning right and this will take you to the La Concha beach which is a stunning sight to behold. It is a superb place for capturing amazing photographs, but the currents make it too dangerous to swim. Now head south into the interior of the island along a path that

OTHER TITLES

La Graciosa

A collection of photographs of the island taken by documentalists Nick and Elza Wagner in the 1970s.

La isla de Alegranza

Written by Agustín Pallarés, resident on the island for more than 40 years, this book details Alegranza and its natural treasures and chronicles the legendary life of the lighthouse keepers of this islet.

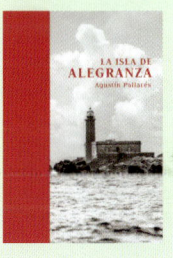

The island of La Graciosa

PEDRO BARBA

The second settlement on the island of La Graciosa was established in 1930 by people who had moved across from Lanzarote. The town grew to a population of approximately 100 and it even had its own school. Then the 1960s saw its decline and by 1960 the last family had moved out. The hamlet was then purchased by a group of people from Gran Canaria who turned Pedro Barba into a place for holiday homes and it has remained as such since then.

takes you between Montaña de Las Agujas and Montaña del Mojón. Stick to this path going south until you reach Caleta del Sebo where you can stop and have a dip at the harbour beach before enjoying some delicious fresh fish in one of the local restaurants.

Alternative route

Head north out of Pedro Barba along the dirt road until you reach the fork and this time go straight ahead, up a slight slope which veers west. This walk takes you around the south side of the cluster of Las Agujas volcanoes and then to the central part of the island which is the only farming area of La Graciosa. On the side of the Montaña Aguja Grande (the tallest mountain on the island at 266 metres) you can see where volcanic *toba* rocks were extracted in the past to construct houses and other buildings. Turn left for the main sandy track that runs between the north and south of the island and head back to Caleta del Sebo harbour.

Recommendations for families

If you are travelling to La Graciosa with young family members, the best option from Caleta del Sebo is to walk southwest past the harbour beach and along a dirt road away from the houses. This leads to some excellent beaches for swimming and lovely walks along the coast to Playa del Salao, Playa Francesa and Playa de la Cocina (next to Montaña Amarilla).

POINTS OF INTEREST

La Graciosa

Formation of this island started some 45,000 years ago and it later experienced an eruptive period of more than 15,000 years which produced some spectacular volcanic cones. The eruptions of Montaña Amarilla were hydromagmatic in the first phase and subaerial in the second phase which accounts for the clear colour differences in this volcano. Historically, La Graciosa was simply a place for passing through as far as human activity was concerned, as its lack of water made it uninhabitable. It was good for putting livestock out to pasture, to hunt Cory's shearwaters (*Calonectris diomedea*), to fish and go shellfishing. Indeed, Agustín de Herrera y Rojas, the marquis of Lanzarote granted the people of Lanzarote free use of the island for such purposes. Towards the end of the 19th century building began on a fish salting factory in La Graciosa (funded by *Pesquerías Canario-Africanas*) and even though the company went bust, the people that had moved over to the island to work in the factory remained, and over time the Caleta del Sebo area evolved into the main hub of the island. The local population gradually increased over the years and by the 1960s approximately 600 people had made the island their home. Then the recession and the downward trend set in and numbers decreased for many years until the 1990s when they started to increase again to the 670 inhabitants it now has.

The people of La Graciosa have long earned their livelihoods from fishing, which is still the case today, although nowadays tourism has become an important part of local life and a source of valuable income.

Marine Reserve

The Marine Reserve of La Graciosa and the Islets to the north of Lanzarote was created in 1995 in accordance with Decree 51 of 26th April 1995 and Ministerial Order 131 of June 2nd 1995. It comprises an area of 70,700 hectares with 60% being internal waters and 40% territorial waters. This protection of the sea is divided into several zones, one is the integrated reserve area where fishing is prohibited within a mile radius of the Roque del Este rock and in the rest of the Reserve fishing is also strictly regulated and policed.

PART III

MUSEUMS AND CENTRES OF INTEREST

ÓRZOLA:
- **Pardelas Park**
Children's Farm & Recreation Park
La Quemadita, 88
Tel. 928 842 545
www.pardelas-park.com
- **Lanzaloe Farm-Museum**
La Quemadita, 96
Tel. 902 362 258
Open Monday to Friday 10.30 am
- 5.30 pm
www.lanzaloe.com

HARÍA:
- **Sacred Art Museum**
Haría Square. Open Tuesday,
Thursday & Saturday 9 am - 3 pm
Tel. 629 591 690
- **César Manrique House-Museum**
Calle César Manrique
Tel.928 843 138
Open daily 10.30 am - 2 pm
www.fcmanrique.org
- **Municipal Farmers Market**
Calle La Longuera, Haría
www.ayuntamientodeharia.com
- **Art & Craft Market**
Haría Square
Saturdays 10 am - 2.30 pm
www.ayuntamientodeharia.com
- **El Ajibe Art Gallery, Haría**
Local art gallery located next to
Haría town hall.
www.ayuntamientodeharia.com

OTHER PLACES OF INTEREST IN THE AREA:
- Centre of Art, Culture and
Tourism in Lanzarote
www.cactlanzarote.com
- **Mirador del Río**
Main road to Ye, LZ-202
Tel. 928 526 548
Open Monday to Sunday
10 am - 5.45 pm (till 6.45 pm from
July - September)
- **Cueva de los Verdes
(The Greens' Caves)**
LZ-204
Tel. 928 848 484
Open Monday to Sunday 10 am
- 6 pm (till 7 pm from July -
September)

- **Jameos del Agua**
LZ-204
Tel. 928 848 020
Open Monday to Sunday 10 am - 6 pm (until 10.30 pm on Saturdays in autumn and till midnight on Saturdays from July - September).

ARRIETA:
- **Lanzarote Aloe Museum**
C/ El Cortijo 2, Arrieta
Tel. 928 848 203
Open Monday to Friday 11 am - 7 pm
www.aloepluslanzarote.es/museo

GUATIZA:
- **Jardín de Cactus (Cactus Garden)**
Avd. Garafía s/n. Guatiza
Tel. 928 529 397
Open daily 10 am - 5.45 pm (from 9 am July - September)
www.cactlanzarote.com
- **Guatiza Salt Works**
Los Cocoteros.
Tel. 615 245 540
www.saldelanzarote.com

TEGUISE:
- **Nuestra señora de Guadalupe Church**
Plaza de La Constitución square
Open Monday to Friday 10 am - 1 pm
- **Palacio Spínola. Timple Museum**
Plaza de la Constitución
Tel. 928 845 181
Open Monday to Friday 9.00 am - 4 pm. Open Sundays & public holidays 9.00 am - 3 pm
www.casadeltimple.org
- **The San Francisco Diocesan Museum of Sacred Art**
Plaza de San Francisco
Calle José Betancor
Tel. 646 879 955
Open Tuesday to Saturday 9.30 am - 4.30 pm. Sunday 10.am - 2 pm
- **Teguise Historical Archive**
Tel. 928 845 467
Open Monday to Friday 8 am - 3 pm
- **Pirate Museum**
Santa Bárbara Castle on Mount Guanapay
Tel. 686 470 376
Open daily 10 am - 4 pm
www.museodelapirateria.com
- **El Faro Cheesemakers**
at km 4.2 on the LZ-30
Teguise-Mozaga road
Tel. 928 521 408
www.queseriaelfaro.es

TESEGUITE:
- **Pottery Studio & Workshop**
Avenida Acorán, 47
Tel. 928 845 650
Open Monday to Friday 11 am - 5 pm
www.aguttenberger.com
www.lanzarote-ceramic.eu

NAZARET:
- **Lagomar Museum**
Calle Los Loros, 2
Tel. 672 461 555 - 928 845 460
Open daily 10 am - 6 pm
www.lag-o-mar.com

SAN BARTOLOMÉ:
- **Tanit Ethnograhic Museum**
Calle Constitución, 1
Tel. 928 802 549. Open Monday to Friday 10 am - 2 pm
www.museotanit.com
- **Casa Ajei**
Calle César Manrique
www.sanbartolome.es

- **San Bartolomé Town Square, Theatre and Church**
Plaza León y Castillo
www.sanbartolome.es
- **Casa Mayor Guerra**
Calle Serpiente
www.sanbartolome.es
- **José María Gil Windmill**
Calle José Maria Gil, 4

TAHÍCHE:
- **César Manrique Foundation**
Taro de Tahíche
Tel. 928 843 138
Open Monday - Saturday and public holidays 9 am - 6 pm.
Sunday 9 am - 3 pm
www.fcmanrique.org

MONTAÑA BLANCA:
- **Guatisea Water Reservoirs**
At the entrance to the town, take the Calle San Bartolomé road and they are located on the north side of Mount Guatisea.
- **Montaña Blanca Water Reservoirs**
Located on the south side of Montaña Blanca.
- **Montaña Blanca Cheesemakers**
Calle Las Rosas, 21
Tel. 928 520 817
Open 9 am - 2 pm
- **El Especiero Cheesemakers**
Calle el Especiero
Tel. 629 384 860
- **Senderismo Lanzarote (Lanzarote Hiking head office)**
Tel. 690 053 282
www.senderismolanzarote.com

TÍAS:
- **La Candelaria Church**
Camino Vistas de Tías lane
Located next to the old Tías cemetery.
- **San Antonio Chapel**
Tías central avenue. Built at the beginning of the 19th century it now houses an art gallery.
- **José Saramago House-Museum**
Calle Los Topes, 3. Tías
Open Monday to Saturday 10 am - 2.30 pm
www.acasajosesaramago.com

TEGOYO:
- **Tegoyo Chapel (19th century)**
LZ-501 main road

UGA:
- **Uga valley**
Camel farms
- **Uga Pottery**
Tel. 928 830 111

YAIZA:
- **Nuestra Señora de los Remedios Church (18th century)**
Plaza de los Remedios square
- **Casa de la Cultura Benito Pérez Armas Cultural Centre**
Plaza Remedios square, 1
www.yaiza.es

MOZAGA:
- **Farmhouse Museum, Lanzarote Art, Cultural & Tourism Centre**
Open Monday to Sunday 10 am - 5.45 pm (open until 6.30 pm

July - September)
www.cactlanzarote.com

ARRECIFE:
- **International Contemporary Art Museum (MIAC), Lanzarote Art, Cultural & Tourism Centre**
Open Monday to Sunday 10 am - 8 pm
www.cactlanzarote.com
- **Arrecife Museum**
Located in the San Gabriel Castle.
www.arrecife.es
- **Arrecife Art Gallery**
Municipal art gallery for exhibitions organised by Arrecife town hall. Located next to the Charco de San Ginés old harbour.
www.arrecife.es

TIAGUA:
- **El Patio Agricultural Museum**
Calle Echeyde, 18
Tel. 928 529 134
Open Monday - Friday
10 am - 5 pm

THE AIRPORT:
- **Aeronautical & Aviation Museum**
Open Monday - Saturday 10 am - 2 pm

MASDACHE:
- **El Grifo Wine Museum**
LZ-30 main road
Open daily 10.30 am - 6pm
www.elgrifo.com

MANCHA BLANCA:
- **Timanfaya Visitors' Centre**
Mancha Blanca, LZ-67 main road.
Tel. 928 118 042
Open Monday - Sunday
9 am - 4 pm
www.reservasparquesnacionales.es
- **Timanfaya National Park/ Fire Mountains**
Open Monday to Sunday 9 am - 5.45 pm (until 6.45 pm July - September)
www.cactlanzarote.com

PUERTO DEL CARMEN:
- **Rancho Texas Park**
Calle Noruega, 35510
Puerto del Carmen
Tel. 928 841 286
www.ranchotexaslanzarote.com

PUERTO CALERO:
- **Puerto Calero Marina**
2nd floor Antiguo Varadero building , 35571 Yaiza, Las Palmas
Tel. 928 510 850
www.puertocalero.com

JANUBIO:
- **Janubio Salt works**
Open 7 am - 2.30 pm
Tel. 928 804 398 - 630 851 383
www.salinasdejanubio.com

FEMÉS:
- **San Marcial del Rubicón Church**
Plaza de Femés square
- **Rubicón Cheesemakers**
Plaza de Femés, 3 square
Tel. 649 911 289

PLAYA BLANCA:
- **Marina Rubicón**
Castillo del Águila,
Calle el Berrugo, 2
Tel. 928 51 90 12
www.marinarubicon.com
- **Los Ajaches Cheesemakers**
Camino de Papagayo
Tel. 678 367 746 – 616 305 527

FOOD & WINES

LA GRACIOSA:
There are plenty of bars and restaurants to choose from on the island of La Graciosa. Most of them can be found around the harbour area, although some are inland, just ask and you'll be pointed in the right direction. The main speciality is, of course, the local catch of the day.

- **El Marinero Restaurant**
Calle García Escámez
Tel. 928 842 070
- **Casa de Comidas Enriqueta**
Calle Mar de Barlovento, 6
Tel. 620 194 592
- **Casa Chano Restaurant- Bar La Caletilla**
Avenida Virgen del Mar
Tel. 928 842 068
- **El Girasol Restaurant**
Calle La Popa, 2
- **Bar El Veril**
Playa de Caleta de Sebo
- **El Varadero Restaurant**
Avenida Virgen del Mar

ÓRZOLA:
Despite its small size, there are many bars and restaurants in this small coastal village. The fresh fish of the day comes highly recommended.

- **Los Gallegos Restaurant**
Calle La Quemadita, 6
Tel. 928 842 502
- **Casa Arráez Restaurant**
Calle Peña Señor Dionisio, 8
Tel. 657 814 885
- **Charco Viejo Restaurant**
Calle La Quemadita, 8
Tel. 928 842 591
- **Punta Fariones Restaurant**
Calle La Quemadita, 10
- **Bahía de Órzola Restaurant**
Calle La Quemadita, 3
Tel. 928 842 575
- **La Perla del Atlántico Restaurant**
Avenida de Órzola
Tel. 928 842 589
- **El Norte Restaurant**
Calle El Embarcadero, 6
- **Pardelas Park Restaurant**

Calle La Quemadita, 88
Tel. 629 042 677
www.pardelas-park-restaurante.com

YE:
Has bars and restaurants where you can stop and have a tapa or some lunch.
- **Volcán de La Corona Restaurant**
Calle Malpaís, 8
- **Yé Social/Cultural Centre**
Calle San Francisco Javier

HARÍA:
Most of the bars and restaurants can be found in and around the main square.
- **Dos Hermanos Restaurant**
Haría Square
Tel. 928 835 409
- **La Tegala Social/Cultural Club**
Haría Square
- **La Frontera Restaurant**
Calle Casa de Atrás, 4
Tel. 928 835 310
  Ney-Ya Café
Haría Square
- **El Rincón de Quino**
Haría Square
- **Puerta Verde Restaurant**
Calle Fajardo
- **El Cortijo Restaurant**
Calle El Palmeral.
Tel. 928 835 686
www.elcortijodeharia.blogspot.com.es

JAMEOS DEL AGUA:
- **Los Jameos del Agua Restaurant**
Tel. 928 848 024

ARRIETA:
Home to plentiful top quality restaurants.
- **El Amanecer Restaurant**
Calle de la Garita, 44
- **El Charcón Restaurant**
Calle El Charcón, 13
Tel. 928 848 110
- **Los Pescaditos Restaurant**
Calle de La Garita, 58
Tel. 928 848 266
- **El Marinero Restaurant**
Calle de la Garita, 60
- **La Nasa Restaurant**
Calle de La Garita, 62
Tel. 928 848 327
-**Bodegas La Grieta winery**
Tel. 928 848 110

TEGUISE:
The Villa de Teguise is home to many unique restaurants which are often located in sensitively converted traditional old houses.
- **Acatife Restaurant**
Calle San Miguel, 4
Plaza de la Constitución
Tel. 928 845 037
- **El Chiringuito Café / Bar**
Calle Reyes Católicos.
- **La Tahona Bar**
Calle Santo Domingo, 3
Tel. 928 845 892
- **La Villa Pizzeria**
Calle José Betancor, 5
Tel. 928 845 904
- **El Sabio Pizzeria**
Calle Santo Domingo
- **Cejas Café / Bar**
Plaza de San Francisco, 5
Tel. 928 845 101
- **Cafetería San Miguel**
Callejón de La Sangre
Tel. 630 733 536
- **El Patio Creperie**
Calle Duende, 1
Tel. 928 845 859
- **Biohespérides Restaurant**
Calle León y Castillo, 3. Casa León
Tel. 928 59 48 64

- **La Cantina Restaurant**
Calle León y Castillo, 8
Tel 928 84 55 36
- **Ikarus Restaurant**
Calle 18 Julio
- **La Bodeguita del Medio Bar**
Plaza Clavijo y Fajardo

COSTA TEGUISE:
This tourist resort offers a wide variety of restaurants, including some renowned top quality establishments.
- **Isla Bonita**
Avenida del Mar
Tel. 928 591 526
- **Villa Toledo**
Avenida Los Cocederos
Tel. 928 346 257
- **La Jordana Restaurant**
Calle Los Geranios
Tel. 928 590 328
- **Neptuno Restaurant**
Avenida del Jablillo
Tel. 928 590 378
- **La Masía Restaurant**
Avenida del Golf
Tel. 928 592 556
- **El Bocadito Bar**
Centro Comercial Los Charcos Shopping Centre
Tel. 928 346 794
Tel. 928 346 794

CALETA DE FAMARA:
This small fishing village offers places where you can sample fresh fish, and local wines as you admire the stunning views across Famara beach set against the backdrop of its dramatic cliffs.
- **El Risco Restaurant**
Calle Montaña Clara, 30
Tel. 928 52 85 50
www.restauranteelrisco.com

- **El Sol Restaurant**
Calle Salvavidas
Tel. 928 528 788
www.restaurantesolfamara.com
- **Casa García Restaurant**
Avenida Marinero, 1
Tel. 928 528 710
- **Famara Social /Cultural Club**

ARRECIFE:
- **Casa Ginory**
Calle Juan Quesada, 9
Tel. 928 811 910
- **Leito de Proa Bar / Restaurant**
Charco de San Ginés harbour
- **Chef Nizar**
Calle Luís Morote
Tel. 928 801 260
- **Bar Andalucía**
Calle Inspector Luís Martín
- **San José (Contemporary Art Museum) Restaurant**
Avenida de Naos
Tel. 928 812 321
- **San Ginés Fisherman's Co-op Restaurant**
Avenida de Naos
- **Bar Restaurante El Molino**
Avenida de Naos
Tel. 928 811 587

- **Asturias Bar**
Avenida Mancomunidad, 5
www.barasturiasarrecife.com
- **Los Conejeros Bar**
Calle Rafael Gonzalez Negrín, 9
Tel. 928 817 195
- **Museo del Vino Bar**
Calle García de Hita, 8

SAN BARTOLOMÉ:
- **Bar el Moreno**
Calle El Quintero, 24
Tel. 928 520 287
- **Bar La Avenida**
Av. Alcalde Antonio Cabrera
- **Café Barreto**
Av. Alcalde Antonio Cabrera, 20
Tel. 928 520 155
- **La Bolera**
Calle Cervantes, 3
- **La Barraca Bar / Restaurant**
Calle Rubicón, 12
Tel. 928 520 558
- **La Plaza Bar**
Next to the town hall.
- **Lo Nuestro Bar**
Calle Guadarfía, 3

MOZAGA:
- **Caserío de Mozaga Rural Hotel and Restaurant**
Calle Malva, 8
Tel. 928 520 060
- **Monumento del Campesino**
Tel. 928 52 01 36
- **Durán de Mozaga Social / Cultural Club**

NAZARET:
- **Lagomar Restaurant**
www.lag-o-mar.com

MONTAÑA BLANCA:
- **Tasca Mi Garaje**
Calle Las Rosas, 48

TÍAS:
- **La Esquina Pizzeria**
Avenida Central, 37
Tel. 928 83 39 67
- **La Ermita Café / Bar**
Avenida Central, 63
Tel. 928 52 40 76
www.cafelaermita.com
- **Taberna Iguad**
Avenida Central, 73
Tel. 928 83 30 93
- **Millo y Millo Arepas**
Calle Libertad, 23
Tel. 928 834 377

PUERTO DEL CARMEN:
- **La Cascada del Puerto Restaurant**
Calle Roque Nublo, 5
Tel. 928 512 953
- **La Casa Roja Restaurant**
Calle Varadero, 22
Tel. 928 515 866
- **Puerto Bahía Restaurant**
Avenida del Varadero, 5
Tel. 928 513 793
- **Puerto Viejo Restaurant**
Avenida del Varadero

CONIL:
- **Aday Social/Cultural Centre**
Tías - Conil main road
- **Bar Casa Juan Ramón - Los Lechoncitos**
Tías-Conil main road. Number 42

LA ASOMADA:
- **Achimencey Social/Cultural Centre**
Mácher - La Asomada main road

MÁCHER:
- **La Tegala Restaurant**
Tías-Yaiza main road. Number 60
Tel. 928 514 524

MASDACHE:
- **El Grifo Winery**
LZ-30 main road San Bartolomé - Masdache
www.elgrifo.com
Tel. 928 524 036
- **Masdache Social/Cultural Centre**
LZ-30 main road
Tel. 690 939 292
- **Vega de Yuco Winery**
Camino del Cabezo
Tel. 928 524 316
www.vegadeyuco.es

LA FLORIDA:
- **Los Bermejos Winery**
Camino Los Bermejos, 7
Tel. 928 522 463
www.losbermejos.com
- **La Florida Winery**
LZ- 30 main road. Tel. 928 593 001

LA GERIA:
- **La Geria Winery**
LZ-30 main road
Tel. 928 173 178
www.lageria.com
- **Rubicón Winery**
LZ- 30 main road
Tel. 928 173 708
www.bodegasrubicon.com
- **Stratvs Winery**
LZ-30 main road
Tel. 928 809 977
- **El Chupadero Winery**
LZ-30 main road

TAO:
- **El Bodegón de Tao**
Calle Adargoma, 28
Tel. 620 927 136
- **El Fomento Social/Cultural Centre. Bar/Restaurant**
Calle Achimencey, 25
Tel. 696 570 863

TINAJO:
- **Casa Ignacio Restaurant**
Avenida de Los Volcanes, 14
Tel. 928 838 003

MANCHA BLANCA:
- **El Diablo Restaurant**
Timanfaya National Park
- **La Mareta Bar**
Calle Chimanfaya.
- **Reymar Winery**
Plaza de Los Dolores, 19
Tel. 928 840 737

TINGUATÓN:
-**Grill Tinguatón**
Calle Tinguatón, 22
Tel. 625 692 009

TIAGUA:
- **El Tenique Bar / Restaurant**
Tiagua - Tinajo main road
Tel. 928 529 856

LA VEGUETA:
- **Mesón Grill Las Cadenas**
La Vegueta - Mancha Blanca main road
Tel. 928 840 443

UGA:
- **Huerta Vieja - Casa Juan Bar / Restaurant**
Calle Malagueña, 2
Tel. 928 830 090
- **Casa Gregorio Bar / Restaurant**
Calle Joaquín Rodríguez
Tel. 928 830 108
- **La Cantosa Café / Burger Bar**
Calle Joaquín Rodríguez, 16
Tel. 928 830 468
- **La Bodega de Uga Winery Bar / Restaurant**
Arrecife - Yaiza main road
Tel. 928 83 01 47

YAIZA:

- **Bodega de Santiago Restaurant**
Calle Montañas del Fuego, 23
Tel. 928 836 204
- **La Era Restaurant**
Calle El Barranco, 2
Tel. 928 830 016
- **Stop Bar**
Next to the Los Remedios church.
Calle Vista de Yaiza.
- **La Casona de Yaiza Restaurant**
Calle Valle de Fenauso, 11
Tel. 928 836 262

PUERTO CALERO:

- **Amura Restaurant**
on marina promenade
Tel. 928 513 181
- **Puro Gusto Foccacia/Pizza Restaurant**
Antiguo Varadero building in the marina.
- **El Tomate Restaurant**
on marina promenade
Tel. 928 512 210
- **Minato Sushi Bar**
Antiguo Varadero building in the marina. Tel. 928 944 190
www.sushibarminatolanzarote.com

EL GOLFO:

- **Costa Azul Restaurant**
Calle Timón, 8
Tel. 928 173 199
- **Casa Torano**
Avenida Marítima de El Golfo, 40
Tel 928 173 058
- **El Golfo Restaurant**
Avenida Marítima de El Golfo, 8
Tel. 928 173 147
- **El Caletón Restaurant**
Avenida Marítima de El Golfo, 66
- **Mar Azul Restaurant**
Avenida Marítima de El Golfo, 48

- **El Bogavante Restaurant**
Av Marítima, 39
Tel. 928 17 35 05

LAS BREÑAS:

- **Los Tres Bar/Supermarket**
- **Casa Marcos Restaurant**
Calle La Cancela, 6

PLAYA BLANCA:

There is a wide range of restaurants, cafés and bars in this resort, offering something for everyone.
- **Casa José R estaurant**
Plaza de Nuestra Señora del Carmen, 5
Tel. 928 518 466
- **Brisa Marina Restaurant**
Avenida Marítima
Tel. 928 517 206
- **El Tonel Restaurant**
Calle Complejo Costa Roja. Local B
Tel. 682 775 515
- **El Almacén de la Sal Restaurant**
Avenida Marítima, 20
Tel. 928 517 885
- **Isla de Lobos Restaurant**
Hotel Princesa Yaiza
Tel. 928 519 222
- **Playa Blanca Fisherman's Co-op Restaurant**
Located in the harbour itself
Tel. 928 518 466
- **La Bocaina Restaurant**
Calle Varadero, 4
- **La Casa Roja Restaurant**
Puerto Marina Rubicón
Tel. 928 51 96 44

ACCOMMODATION

THROUGHOUT THE ISLAND:
- **www.rural-villas.com**
Tel. 619 231 904
Luxury villas and houses all over the island.
- **www.villasdelanzarote.com**
Villas and houses across the island.

LA GRACIOSA:
There are a number of apartments available to rent. Free camping is also possible in El Salado with bookings made online via www.reservasparquesnacionales.es
- **Pensión Enriqueta Guesthouse**
Tel. 928 842 051
- **Pensión Girasol Playa Guesthouse**
- **La Graciosa Apartments**
www.apartamentoslagraciosa.com
Tel. 635 797 156
- **La Pardela Apartments**
www.apartamentoslapardela.com
Tel. 928 987 037
- **El Sombrerito Apartments**
www.elsombrerito.com
Tel. 696 942 874
- **Casa Nely**
www.villasdelanzarote.com

ÓRZOLA:
Apartments can be rented privately; it's best to ask around locally for further details.
- **Charco de La Pared Apartments**
Calle Charco de La Pared, 20
Tel. 928 812 791
- **Pardelas Park**
Órzola - Ye main road.
This farm and recreation park offers camping facilities for groups. Breakfast, lunch and dinner are also available.
Tel. 928 842 545
www.pardelas-park.com

YE:
- **La Corona Rural Hotel**
Calle Las Rositas 8
Tel. 619 231 904
www.rural-villas.com

MÁGUEZ:
There is hostel with dormitory-type accommodation run by the

island council, the *Cabildo*. Caters for educational visits and groups.
- **Aula de la naturaleza de Maguez**
www.auladenaturalezademaguez.com
- **Casa La Ermita**
Tel. 928 842 535 - 659 021 447
www.casalaermita.com

HARÍA:
There are rural houses and apartments available for rentals. Enquire locally for up-to-date information.
- **Finca La Crucita**
Calle San Juan, 63
www.villasdelanzarote.com
- **Villa Lola y Juan**
Calle Fajardo, 16
www.villalolayjuan.com

ARRIETA Y PUNTA MUJERES:
There are a number of apartments and houses available for holiday lets in both towns.
- **House and Apartment Rentals**
www.villasdelanzarote.com
- **Arrieta Apartments**
Tel. 928 848 230 - 606 176 028

TABAYESCO:
- **Finca de Arrieta**
Carretera Arrieta-Tabayesco, s/n.
Tel. 928 826 720
- **Finca Las Quentia**
Calle Chafariz, 1
Tel. 606 956 121

MALA:
- **Casa Helma**
Calle Cercado
Tel. 928 52 95 41
www.casahelma.com

TESEGUITE:
- **Finca Luna**
Calle Gamona, 21
fincaluna@eliotropo.eu
- **Casa Teseguite**
Av. Acorán, 55
Tel. 619 042 422

TEGUISE:
- **Chimidas House/Studio**
Calle Jaime Balmes, 14
Tel. 928 593 013
www.estudiochimida.com

FAMARA:
- **Finca Las Laderas Rural House**
Carretera Las Laderas, 2
Tel. 928 173 942
www.fincalanzarote.de

LOS VALLES:
- **Casitas Los Valles**
Calle Zorrocloco, 31
Tel. 928 528 104
646 937 989
- **Casa Catalina**
Calle San Isidro Labrador, 12
Tel. 619 231 904
www.rural-villas.com
- **Casa El Aljibe**
Calle San Isidro Labrador, 12
Tel. 619 231 904
www.rural-villas.com
- **Casa Barranco.**
Calle Bentaiga, 3
Tel. 619 231 904
www.rural-villas.com

SOO:
- **La Casa Blanca**
Calle Los Parranderos, 3
Tel. 928 526 140
606 029 028
www.lacasablanca.org

SAN BARTOLOMÉ:
- **Casa José Manuel**
Calle César Manrique
Tel. 646 656 230

LA FLORIDA:
- **La Florida Rural Hotel**
Calle El Parral, 1
Tel. 928 521 124
www.hotelfincalaflorida.com

EL ISLOTE:
- **Casa El Alpende**
Calle El Parral, 14
Tel. 620 387 727
www.casaruralelalpende.es
- **Casa Tomar**
Calle El Parral, 144
Tel. 928 522 618
www.tomaren.com

MOZAGA:
- **Caserío de Mozaga**
Calle Malva, 8
Tel. 928 520 060
info@caseriodemozaga.com
www.caseriodemozaga.com
- **Finca Isabel**
Calle Malvas, 11
Tel. 609 742 163.
www.fincaisabel.com

MONTAÑA BLANCA:
For apartments contact:
Tel. 690 053 282

MASDACHE:
- **Finca Fajardo**
Camino el Mentidero, 6
Tel. 669 102 426

TÍAS:
- **La Orilla Rural House**
Calle San Blas, 6
Tel. 928 810 832

- **Casa Las Claras**
C/ Camino de las Claras, 13
Tel. 928 834 330

LA ASOMADA:
- **Casa Gaida**
Camino La Caldereta, 52
Tel. 928 832 531 - 629 731 441
www.casagaida.com

UGA:
- **Casa El Morro**
Calle El Morro, 1
Tel. 699 417 871
www.casaelmorro.com

YAIZA:
- **La Casona de Yaiza Hotel / Restaurant**
Calle Valle de Fenauso, 11
Tel. 928 836 262
www.casonadeyaiza.com
- **Casa de Hilario**
Calle Los Rostros, 5
Tel. 928 836 262

LA SANTA:
There are some apartments available for holiday lets in La Santa village but the Club La Santa Sports hotel is the main place for accommodation in Tinajo.
- **Club La Santa**
Tel. 928 599 999
www.clublasanta.es

TISALAYA:
- **Finca Tisalaya**
Camino de Tisalaya, 1
Tel. 928 177 976 - 676 231 223

COSTA TEGUISE:
One of the island's three main resorts and probably the quietest and tidiest. It also has lots of gardens and green spaces to enjoy.

- **Hotel Gran Meliá Salinas**
Tel. 928 590 040
www.melia.com
- **Beatriz Costa Teguise**
Calle Atalaya, 3
Tel. 928 590 828
www.beatrizhoteles.com
- **Occidental Allegro Oasis**
Avenida del Mar
Tel. 928 590 410
- **Occidental Grand Teguise Playa**
Avenida del Jablillo
Tel. 928 590 654

ARRECIFE:

There is not a vast amount of holiday accommodation available in the island's capital, but the Arrecife Gran Hotel has become a well-known landmark as the capital's tallest building.
- **Arrecife Gran Hotel**
Tel. 928 800 000
www.arrecifehoteles.com
- **Hotel Lancelot**
Tel. 928 805 099
www.hotellancelot.com
- **Hotel Miramar**
Tel. 928 801 522
www.hmiramar.com

PUERTO DEL CARMEN:

As the island's first tourist resort and therefore its most established, Puerto del Carmen offers a wide variety of accommodation throughout the resort.
- **Hotel Los Fariones**
Calle Roque del Este, 1
Tel. 928 510 175
www.farioneshotels.com
- **Hotel San Antonio**
Avenida de las playas
Tel. 928 514 200
- **Apartamentos Fariones**
Calle Timanfaya, 8
Tel. 928 55 00 10

www.grupofariones.com
- **Hotel Beatriz Playa**
Tel. 928 512 166
www.beatrizhoteles.com
- **Pensión Magec**
Calle Hierro, 8
Tel. 928 513 874
- **Hotel La Geria**
Calle Júpiter, 5
Tel 928 511 041

PUERTO CALERO:

This marina offers select accommodation facilities on the eastern coast of the island.
- **Hotel Hesperia Lanzarote**
Tel. 928 080 800
www.hesperia.es
- **Hotel Costa Calero**
Tel. 928 849 595
www.hotelcostacalero.com
- **Villas Puerto Calero**
Tel. 928 849 539
www.villaspuertocalero.com

PLAYA BLANCA:

With one of the largest coasts on Lanzarote, Playa Blanca is the resort that has experienced the most recent expansion thanks to the tourism boom. Visitors can choose from a variety of accommodation including, 5-star hotels, villas and self-catering apartment complexes.
- **Hotel Volcán Lanzarote**
Urb. Castillo del Aguila
Tel. 928 519 185
- **Hotel Princesa Yaiza**
Av. del Papagayo, s/nTel. 928 519 222

TRANSPORT

BUS SERVICE
- **Regular bus service**
Intercitybus
Tel. 928 811 522
www.intercitybuslanzarote.es

TAXI SERVICE
- **Taxis in San Bartolomé & Lanzarote Airport**
Tel. 630 207 305 - 928 520 176
www.lanzarotetaxi.com
- **Taxis in Arrecife**
Tel. 928 800 806 - 902 363 400
www.taxipuertodearrecife.com
www.taxidearrecife.com
- **Taxis in Haría**
Tel. 620 315 350
- **Taxis in Teguise**
Tel. 928 524 223
- **Taxis in Tías**
Tel. 928 524 220
- **Taxis in Tinajo**
Tel. 928 840 049
- **Taxis in Yaiza**
Tel. 928 524 222

BOAT SERVICE
- **Ferry service to the island of Fuerteventura**
- Naviera Armas
Tel. 902 456 500
www.navieraarmas.com
- Fred Olsen
Tel. 902 100 107
www.fredolsen.es
- Líneas Romero
Tel. 928 596 107
www.lineasromero.com
- **Ferry service to La Graciosa**
- Líneas Romero
Tel. 928 842 055
www.lineasromero.com
- Biosfera Express
Tel. 928 84 25 85
www.biosferaexpress.com

CAR HIRE
- **CICAR**
Tel. 928 822 900
www.cicar.com
- **Cabrera Medina**
www.cabreramedina.com

USEFUL WEBSITES

LOCAL COUNCILS
www.cabildodelanzarote.com
www.ayuntamientodeharia.es
www.teguise.es
www.arrecife.es
www.sanbartolome.es
www.tinajo.es
www.ayuntamientodetias.es
www.yaiza.es

GASTRONOMY
www.saborealanzarote.org
www.dolanzarote.com
www.comerenlanzarote.com

EVENTS, SPORTS & LEISURE
www.senderismolanzarote.com
www.senderosatlanticos.com
www.lanzarotewinerun.com
www.sonidosliquidos.com
www.turismolanzarote.com
www.lanzarotedeportes.com
www.lanzarotenbici.com
www.ironmanlanzarote.com
www.masdeporteslanzarote.com
www.masscultura.com
www.ociolanzarote.com

CULTURE & TRADITION
www.edicionesremotas.com
www.artesaníadelanzarote.com
www.cactlanzarote.com
www.memoriadelanzarote.com
www.agrolanzarote.com
www.lanzarotebiosfera.org
lanzaroteinedita.blogspot.com.es
agustinpallares.blogspot.com.es

EMERGENCY TELEPHONE NUMBERS

- **Casualty Department and A&E**
Tel. 112
- **Hospital Doctor José Molina Orosa**
Tel. 928 595 000
- **Hospiten Lanzarote**
Tel. 928 59 61 00
- **Civil Guard police**
Tel. 928 592 100
- **National police**
Tel. 928 597 107
- **Consortium of Emergency Services**
Tel. 080

INDEX TO PLACES OF INTEREST

Place	Page
Alfonso Spínola	149
Ana Viciosa Cave	103
Ángel Guerra	148
Archipelago Chinijo	140
Benito Pérez Armas Cultural Centre	89
Bodega El Grifo Winery	98
Bosquecillo Forest	111
Brief History of Haría	72
Brief History of Teguise	81 & 147
Brief History of San Bartolomé	81
Brief history of barrilla saltwort (common iceplant)	82
Caleta de Famara cove	110
Camels on Lanzarote	91
César Manrique	67
City of Rubicón	189
Cueva Paloma Archaeological Site	183
Diama Archaeological Site in La Geria	177
El Río Gun Battery	137
Ermita de la Caridad Chapel	174

Ermita de Las Nieves Chapel	74
Ermita de San Antonio Chapel, Tías	80
Famara spring and water galleries	111
Femés	183
Guardilama Canals	177
Guatisea water reservoirs	157
Guatisea Archaeological Site	83
Islote Rises	160
Janubio Salt Works	124
La Candelaria Church, Tías	80
La Encarnación Church	74
La Graciosa	195
La Graciosa & Los Islotes Marine Reserve	195
La Santa Salt marsh	105
Los Agujeros Salt Works	117
Los Ajaches Natural Monument	189
Los Naturalistas (Las Palomas) Caves	103
Los Volcanes Natural Park	170
Mararía, by Rafael Arozarena	183
Márques de Herrera y Rojas House-Museum	144
Montaña Blanca water reservoirs	157
Mirador del Río	137
Montaña Blanca Archaeological Site	83
Montaña Blanca Cheesemakers	83
Mount Corona Natural Monument	67 & 134
Nuestra Señora de Los Dolores Church	101
Nuestra Señora de Los Remedios Church	94
Orchella weed	140
Paleontological site in Órzola	67
Pechiguera Lighthouse	120
Pedro Barba	194
Pelotamano handball	151
Pollo de Uga Canarian wrestler	89
Protected Landscape of La Geria	157 & 177
Ramalina strap lichen	171
San José Chapel and Farmstead Ruins	73
San Juan de Haría Church	74
San Marcial Church	182
San Roque Church	101
Santo Domingo Convent	144
Sweet potato Cultivation	82
The Diabletes Devils	146
The Legend of Ico	147
Timanfaya National Park	131
Virgin of Guadalupe	150

INDEX TO FLORA

Scientific name	Common name and page reference nº
Acacia cyclops	Red-eyed wattle p.72, 75, 109 & 111
Aeonium lancerottense	Endemic verode succulent p.45, 70, 72 & 108
Agave americana	Agave p.72 & 109
Agave fourcroydes	Henequen p.72 & 109
Ajuga iva	Bugleweed/Carpetbugle p.51
Aloe vera	Aloe vera p.63
Androcymbium psammofilum	Cup and saucer plant p.186
Argyranthemum maderense	Famara daisy p.41, 46, 70, 72, 108 & 111
Arthrocnemum fruticosum	Glasswort p.105
Arundo donax	Spanish cane p.175
Asteriscus intermedius	Yellow-flowering sea daisy (Tojio) p.43, 70 & 111
Asteriscus schultzii	White-flowering sea daisy (Tojio) p.51
Astydamia latifolia	Canary sea fennel p.53, 105 & 192
Bituminaria bituminosa	Arabian pea/ Pitch trefoil p.10, 47, 70, 72 & 108
Cakile maritima	Sea rocket p.53, 186 & 192
Carlina salicifolia	Carlina salicifolia thistle p.70
Cenchrus ciliaris	African foxtail grass p.44, 180 & 186
Convolvulus lopezsocasi	Famara convolvulus p.72 & 109
Cyperus capitatus	Canary sedge p.53
Echium famarae	Famara bugloss p.46
Echium lancerottense	Lanzarote bugloss (Cow's tongue) p.50
Erica arborea	Myrica Erica tree heath p.41
Euphorbia balsamifera	Balsamiferous spurge p.10, 40, 42, 62, 110, 120 & 130
Euphorbia paralias	Sea spurge p.53 & 192
Euphorbia regis jubae	Prickle-leaved (bitter) spurge p.42, 62, 134, 140 & 180
Ferula lancerottensis	Lanzarote fennel p.47, 70, 72 & 108
Ficus carica	Fig tree p.172

Foeniculum vulgare	Fennel p.72 & 109
Forsskaolea angustifolia	Mousetrap nettle p.48
Helianthemum canariense	Canary helianthemum (Rock rose) p.50
Helichrysum monogynum	Lanzarote red helichrysum p.48
Heliotropium ramosissimun	Wavy heliotrope (Camel's tongue) p.49
Ipomoea batatas	Sweet potato p.82
Kleinia neriifolia	Verode (kleinia) p.42, 62 & 130
Launaea arborescens	Barbed-wire bush p.43, 82, 95, 130, 131, 176 & 186
Lavandula pinnata	Lavender p.47 & 140
Licium intricatum	Sea thorn bush p.44, 95, 120, 130 & 180
Lobularia canariensis	White-flowering alyssum p.51
Lotus lancerottensis	Lanzarote trefoil lotus p.48 & 168
Mesembryanthemun crystallinum	Barrilla saltwort (common iceplant) p.19, 44, 82 & 147
Mesembryanthemun nodiflorum	Slenderleaf iceplant p.45
Myrica faya	Firetree shrub p.41
Morus nigra	Black mulberry p.172
Nicotiana glauca	Tree tobacco p.50 & 180
Olea cerasiformis	Canary wild olive tree p.75, 109 & 111
Ononis hesperia	Canary restharrow p.186
Opuntia dillenii	Prickly pear cactus p.180
Opuntia ficus indica	Barbary fig p.116
Pelargonium capitatum	Rose geranium p.168
Phoenix canariense	Canarian palm tree p.40, 49, 69, 134, 163 & 174
Phytolacca dioica	Ombu tree p.91
Pinus halepensis	Aleppo pine tree p.75 & 109
Pinus canariensis	Canary pine tree p.75 & 109
Polycarpaea nivea	Common white saladillo p.176 & 186
Pulicaria canariensis	Canarian fleabane p.45
Ranunculus cortusifolius	Giant buttercup p.70
Rumex lunaria	Canary sorrel p.46, 134, 164, 168 & 176
Salsola tetrandra	Saltwort p.130 & 192
Salsola vermiculata	Mediterranean saltwort p.43, 82, 95, 130 & 192
Schinus molle	Pepper tree p.149
Sarcocornia perennis	Chicken claws p.105
Solanum tuberosum	Potato p.70
Sonchus pinnatifidus	Cliff-dwelling thistle p.49, 72, 108 & 110.
Suaeda vera	Shrubby seablite p.105
Thymus origanoides	Tajosé thyme p.72 & 109
Traganum moquinii	Traganum bush p.52
Zygophyllum fontanesii	Canary sea grape p.52, 105, 192
Vitis vinifera	Grape vine p.172

INDEX TO FAUNA

Scientific name	Common name and page reference nº
Actitis hypoleucos	Common sandpiper p.105
Alectoris barbara	Barbary partridge p.29 & 108
Anthophora sp.	Anthophora fossil p.39 & 192
Anthus berthelotii	Berthelot's pipit p.29, 30, 75 & 109
Ardea cinerea	Grey heron p.29
Arenaria interpres	Ruddy turnstone p.29, 36, 105 & 125
Artemia salina	Brine shrimp p.125
Atelerix algirus	North African hedgehog p.28
Bubulcus ibis	Cattle egret p.29 & 35
Bucanetes githagineus	Trumpeter finch p.29 & 34
Bunochelis spinifera	Opiliones (Harvestman spider) p.39
Burhinus oedicnemus	Stone-curlew p.29 & 34
Calandrella rufescens	Lesser short-toed lark p.29 & 35
Calonectris diomedea	Cory shearwater p.29, 140 & 195
Camelus dromedarius	Dromedary p.90
Carduelis cannabina	Common linnet p.30
Carduelis carduelis	European goldfinch p.29, 75 & 109
Charadrius alexandrinus	Kentish plover p. 37, 105 & 125
Charadrius hiaticula	Common ringed plover p.105 & p.125
Chlamydotis undulata	Canarian Houbara Bustard p.10, 29 & 34
Columba livia	Rock pigeon p.29, 31, 75 & 109

Corvus corax	Common raven p.29 & 32
Crocidura canariensis	Canarian shrew p.28
Cursorius cursor	Cream-coloured courser p.29
Cyanistes teneriffae (Parus caeruleus)	African blue tit p.29, 33, 75 & 109
Dactylopius coccus	Cochineal p.19 & 116
Egretta garzetta	Little egret p.105 & 125
Equus africanus asinus	Donkey p.22
Falco eleonorae	Eleonora's falcon p.29 & 140
Falco pelegrinoides	Barbary falcon p.29, 140 & 165
Falco tinnunculus	Kestrel p.29, 32, 75 & 109
Gallotia atlantica	Atlantic lizard p.28 & 35
Gobius paganellus	Rock goby p.121
Himantopus himantopus	Black-winged stilt p.37 & 125
Lanius meridionalis	Southern grey shrike p.29, 32, 75 & 109
Larus michaellis	Yellow-legged gull p.29, 36 & 120
Munidopsis polymorfa	Blind albino cave crab p.29 & 39
Mus musculus	Common house mouse p.28
Neophron percnopterus	Egyptian vulture p.29 & 140
Numenius phaeopus	Whimbrel p.29, 37, 105 & 125
Oryctolagus cuniculus	European rabbit p.28 & 108
Ovis capra	Goat p.28
Ovis orientalis aries	Sheep p.18
Parablennius parvicornis	Rock-pool blenny p.121
Passer hispaniolensis	Spanish sparrow p.31
Phylloscopus collybita	Common chiffchaff p.29
Physalia physalis	Portuguese man o' war p.38
Platalea leucorodia	Eurasian spoonbill p.105
Pluvialis squatarola	Grey plover p.36, 105 & 125
Rathus sp.	Rat p.28
Ratite	Ratite fossil p.67
Serinus canarius	Canary p.29, 75 & 109
Sphingonotus canariensis	Grasshopper p.38
Sterna sandvicensis	Sandwich tern p.29
Streptopelia decaocto	Collared dove p.31
Sus scrofa	Wild swine p.18
Sylvia conspicillata	Spectacled warbler p.33
Sylvia melanocephala	Sardinian warbler p.33
Tadorna ferruginea	Ruddy shelduck p.125
Tarentola angustimentalis	East Canary wall gecko p.28
Theba geminata	Snail p.38
Tringa nebularia	Common greenshank p 105
Tringa totanus	Common redshank p.105
Upupa epops	Hoopoe / Eurasian hoopoe p.30

SUMMARY OF WALKS

Nº	NAME	DISTANCE	TIMING
1	Órzola - Haría	13 kilometres	3 hrs. 30 m
2	Haría - Teguise	12 kilometres	3 hrs. 30 m
3	Teguise - Tías	15 kilometres	4 hrs.
4	Tías - Yaiza	13.5 kilometres	3 hrs. 30 m
5	Yaiza - Playa Blanca	13.3 kilometres	3 hrs. 30 m
6	Pto. del Carmen - La Santa	28 kilometres	7 hrs.
7	Arrieta - Haría - Famara	16 kilometres	5 hrs. 30 m
8	Costa Teguise - Arrieta	18 kilometres	4 hrs. 30 m
9	Playa Blanca - Janubio	13 kilometres	4 hrs.
10	Timanfaya Coastline	12 kilometres	4 hrs. 30 m
11	Volcán de La Corona	3 kilometres	1 hr. 30 m
12	The People of La Graciosa's Trail	7 kilometres	3 hrs.
13	Historical Teguise	1.2 kilometres	1 hr.
14	Montaña Blanca	8 kilometres	3 hrs.
15	Caldera Blanca	11 kilometres	4 hrs. 30 m
16	Santa Catalina	9 kilometres	3 hrs. 30 m
17	Caldera de los Cuervos	7 kilometres	2 hrs. 30 m
18	La Geria	9 kilometres	3 hrs.
19	Pico Redondo Peak	6 kilometres	2 hrs. 30 m
20	Papagayo	7.5 kilometres	2 hrs. 30 m
21	La Graciosa	17 kilometres	5 hrs. 30 m

FICUTY	TYPE	DEPARTUTRE POINT	FINISHING POINT
Moderate	Linear	Órzola harbour	Plaza de Haría square
Moderate	Linear	Plaza de Haría square	Plaza de la Constitución
Moderate	Linear	Plaza de la Constitución	La Candelaria church
Moderate	Linear	La Candelaria church	Yaiza church
Moderate	Linear	Yaiza church	Playa Blanca church
Moderate	Linear	Puerto del Carmen	La Santa
Moderate	Linear	Arrieta	Caleta de Famara
Moderate	Linear	Costa Teguise	Arrieta
Easy	Linear	Pechiguera lighthouse	Janubio beach
Challenging	Linear	Playa de la Madera	El Golfo
Easy	Circular	Ye - San Francisco church	
Challenging	Circular	Ye - Calle de Las Rositas street	
Easy	Circular	Teguise - Plaza de La Constitución square	
Moderate	Circular	Plaza de Montaña Blanca square	
Moderate	Circular	Mancha Blanca Cultural Centre	
Easy	Circular	Tinguatón main road	
Easy	Circular	Tinguatón main road next to Caldera de los Cuervos	
Easy	Circular	Ermita de la Caridad chapel	
Moderate	Circular	Femés - Plaza	
Easy	Circular	Playa Blanca - last hotel to the east	
Moderate	Circular	Caleta de Sebo harbour	

MAP GLOSSARY

Spanish	English
Aljibe	Water deposit
Archivo municipal	Municipal archive
Avenida	Avenue
Barranco	Ravine
Bodega	Winery
Calle	Street
Callejón	Alley
Casa del Timple	Timple Museum
Casa Museo	House-Museum
Castillo	Castle
Centro de visitantes	Visitors' centre
Ermita	Chapel
Faro	*Lighthouse*
Hotel abandonado	Abandoned hotel
Iglesia	Church
Mareta	Water storage reservoir
Montaña	Mountain
Museo Agrícola	Farming Museum
Museo	Museum
Palacio	Palace
Playa	Beach
Plaza	Plaza / Square
Presa	Dam
Salina	Salt works
Teatro municipal	Municipal theatre
Timple	Timple (Canarian 5-string plucked instrument)
Vega	Plain
Virgen	Holy Virgin
Volcán	Volcano

With the support of:

Cabildo de Lanzarote Island Council

San Bartolomé Town Hall

Tinajo Town Hall

Teguise Town Hall

Tías Town Hall

With the collaboration of:

Cicar
Viajes La Molina
Viajes Alegranza
Haría Town Hall
Bodegas El Grifo Winery
Yaiza Town Hall

o *ediciones* **remotas**

INDEX WALKS

Nº	NAME
1	Órzola - Haría
2	Haría - Teguise
3	Teguise - Tías
4	Tías - Yaiza
5	Yaiza - Playa Blanca
6	Puerto del Carmen - Tinajo - La Santa
7	Arrieta - Haría - Famara
8	Costa Teguise - Arrieta
9	Playa Blanca - Janubio
10	Timanfaya Coastline
11	The Volcán de La Corona Volcano
12	The People of La Graciosa's Trail
13	Historical Teguise
14	Montaña Blanca
15	Caldera Blanca
16	Santa Catalina
17	Caldera de Los Cuervos and Montaña Colorada
18	La Geria
19	The Pico Redondo Peak - Femés
20	Papagayo
21	The island of La Graciosa

Download the walks onto your mobile device:
www.senderismolanzarote.com